Easy Microwave Preserving

Easy Microwave Preserving

THE SHORTCUT WAY TO
PRESERVE YOUR FAVORITE FOODS

Cynthia Fischborn
and Cheryl Long

Chester, Connecticut

Library of Congress Cataloging-in-Publication Data

Fischborn, Cynthia.
    Easy microwave preserving: the shortcut way to preserve your favorite foods /
by Cynthia Fischborn and Cheryl Long. — 2nd ed.
        p.   cm.
    Includes index.
    ISBN 1-56440-016-6
    1. Food—Preservation. 2. Microwave cookery.   I. Long, Cheryl.   II. Title.
TX601.F58 1992
641.4—dc20   91-32507
                                                                        CIP

Manufactured in the United States of America
First Globe Pequot Edition/First Printing

This book is lovingly dedicated to our mothers,
who gave us our first cooking lessons and,
instead of laughing, encouraged us.

About the Authors

Cynthia Fischborn, formerly a home economics instructor in the Portland, Oregon, public school system, has edited a microwave magazine and several cookbooks. She has also taught at cooking schools in the Northwest and worked with various microwave manufacturers, culinary publications, and food commissions, testing and developing recipes for consumers.

Cheryl Long has written several cookbooks and edited a microwave cooking magazine. She has also spent many years working with Litton Industries and Quasar where she served as microwave coordinator and trainer for cooking-school instructors and home economics teachers. Currently, she teaches microwave cookery at Portland (Ore.) Community College and runs Culinary Arts, Ltd., a specialty cookbook publishing company.

Table of Contents

Preface

The two of us have been enthusiastic microwave cooks, both profes-
sionally and at home, for many years. We've tried to cook almost any-
thing edible in our microwave ovens!

Since one thing generally leads to another, we found ourselves
writing a microwave magazine. There was a surprising response from
our readers to the microwave preserving recipes and tips. Once a
brief local television appearance showing how to make our Easy Low-
sugar Berry Freezer Jam drew more than 500 recipe request letters!

These experiences, along with the urgings of students in our
microwave cooking classes, made us aware of the tremendous need
for a book about microwave preserving. This book is a collection of
our best recipes, tips, and techniques. (It is also, we believe, the first
book on the subject.)

The world of microwave cooking is one of continuing expansion.
New products, techniques, recipes, and, not least of all, break-
throughs in microwave technology continue to take place. Thus, as
our book begins a new chapter in microwave cooking, it is just that —
a beginning. Be assured that we will continue to test and experiment
with both recipes and technology of the future and will, when appropriate, update this book. We would be happy to hear from you on this
subject. Our sincere wish is that you find this cookbook the resource
you have been looking for.

ONE

Introduction to Microwave Preserving

Y ou might be tempted to skip this informational chapter and get right to the recipes. Please don't! We want you to be successful with your microwave preserving recipes, and so in this chapter, we have provided essential information on

◆ How to adjust cooking times to your microwave oven wattage;

◆ Microwave power settings;

◆ What utensils to use for microwave cooking;

◆ Two basic methods for prolonged food storage;

◆ Kitchen wraps;

◆ High-altitude cooking; and

◆ Metric and equivalent measures.

By taking a few minutes to read through this chapter, your microwave preserving experience will be informed, easy, and fun—not confusing. Relax, refer to the charts and directions as needed, and make something wonderful!

TABLE 1

Recipe-timing Adjustment Guide for Microwave Ovens

The recipes in this book have been tested in 650- to 700-watt microwave ovens. If your oven falls within this wattage range, use cooking times as given. Microwave ovens with lower wattage require an increase in cooking time, as shown in the guide below:

650 to 700 Watts *If time is:*	500 to 625 Watts *Add 20%*	400 to 500 Watts *Add 35%*
30 seconds	35 seconds	45 seconds
1 minute	1 minute, 10 seconds	1 minute, 25 seconds
2 minutes	2 minutes, 30 seconds	2 minutes, 45 seconds
5 minutes	6 minutes	7 minutes
10 minutes	12 minutes	14 minutes
15 minutes	18 minutes	20 minutes
20 minutes	24 minutes	27 minutes
30 minutes	36 minutes	41 minutes

Microwave Power Settings

Since there are no standards in the microwave industry for power-setting terminology, we are including the following information to explain the terminology used in this book.

HIGH: 100% power
This setting used to be called "COOK." Used for boiling water and other liquids and for blanching and cooking fresh and frozen fruits and vegetables.

MEDIUM-HIGH: 70% power
Sometimes called "ROAST." Used for many things, such as maintaining a gentler boiling point or cooking more delicate mixtures.

MEDIUM: 50% power
Sometimes called "SIMMER." Gives low, gentle heating for finer-textured foods and for simmering foods.

DEFROST: 30% power
Sometimes the same as "LOW." Primarily used to defrost foods. It can also be used to cook delicate foods.

LOW: 20–25% power
The same as "DEFROST" on some ovens.

WARM: 10% power
This is becoming a common term on most ovens. Ideal for keeping foods warm, proofing bread doughs, and softening butter and cream cheese.

Microwave Cooking Utensils

Using the right utensil can mean the difference between a perfectly prepared recipe or a frustrating cooking experience.

While some of today's microwave ovens are metal-tolerant to some degree, this does not mean that food can be cooked in conventional metal pots and pans. Instead, use glass or Corning ware casseroles and lids, glass mixing bowls, or glass measuring cups, including the extra-large two-quart "batter" bowl. Rigid microwave-safe thermoplastic containers (these should be clearly labeled "for microwave use") can also be used. But do avoid using softer plastics; they cannot withstand the heat from the hot food and can melt, sag, or bubble. Most important of all, make sure that all of your microwave containers are deep enough to prevent boil-overs.

Do not leave metal spoons or conventional thermometers in preserving containers while the microwave oven is operating. Wooden spoons may, if desired, be left in while the oven is operating; be aware, however, that moisture generated in the cooking process will warm the spoon if it is left in for a long period of time. Microwave-safe thermometers or probes may, of course, be left in the container while the oven is operating.

Use of Kitchen Wraps in Microwave Preserving

Plastic wrap is the most preferred and versatile wrap used in microwave cooking. When recipe directions say "cover," plastic wrap may be used in place of a lid. Remember that plastic wrap will trap and hold in all of the steam; it is not porous. Some of the steam must be allowed to escape, however, so that the plastic wrap will not bulge or lie flat on the food. There are two ways to do this:

1. Lift a small (1-inch) section of the plastic wrap at the edge or corner of the bowl or container.

2. Using a toothpick, punch several holes in the center of the plastic after sealing it around the edges of the container.

Note: When removing plastic wrap, be careful to lift the edge farthest away from you, pulling the plastic wrap toward you. This will allow the hot steam to escape away from you into the air. Remember, hot steam can burn!

Waxed paper is semiporous and may be used as a lid or covering for foods that need some moisture held in, but not to the point of steaming. It is good as a splatter shield where a tight-fitting cover is not necessary.

Paper towels and napkins are very porous, allowing steam to pass through while absorbing some excess moisture. Although excellent for reheating bread products, these are not a good choice as a covering for recipes in this book. And remember, do not use towels made from recycled paper; they may contain impurities such as metal particles, which could heat and ignite the paper.

Aluminum foil reflects microwaves (and prevents cooking). It is therefore not a suitable covering for cooking foods.

Boiling-water-bath Process

This conventional method of processing is recommended for canning fruits, pickled vegetables, and tomatoes where a long shelf life is desired. It is not necessary for shorter-term refrigeration or, of course, for freezing.

Bring water to a boil conventionally in a water-bath canner. Immerse filled, sealed jars in boiling water. The water level should be 1 inch or more above the top of the jars. Start counting the processing time as soon as all jars have been added and the water returns to a boil. Boil gently and steadily for the amount of time recommended for each recipe.

At higher altitudes (above 1,000 feet), longer processing times are required (see table below).

For further information or questions about conventional boiling-water-bath processing, contact your local USDA Extension office.

TABLE 2

Boiling-water baths at High Altitudes

Altitude	If Total Cooking Time Is Less than 20 minutes, add:	If Total Cooking Time Is More than 20 minutes, add:
1,000 feet	1 minute	2 minutes
2,000 feet	2 minutes	4 minutes
3,000 feet	3 minutes	6 minutes
4,000 feet	4 minutes	8 minutes
5,000 feet	5 minutes	10 minutes
6,000 feet	6 minutes	12 minutes
7,000 feet	7 minutes	14 minutes
8,000 feet	8 minutes	16 minutes
9,000 feet	9 minutes	18 minutes
10,000 feet	10 minutes	20 minutes

◆ EQUIVALENT MEASURES ◆

Dash	=	2 to 4 drops		
3 teaspoons	=	1 tablespoon	=	½ fluid ounce
4 tablespoons	=	¼ cup	=	2 fluid ounces
16 tablespoons	=	1 cup (½ pint)	=	8 fluid ounces
2 cups	=	1 pint	=	16 fluid ounces
2 pints	=	1 quart	=	32 fluid ounces
4 quarts	=	1 gallon	=	128 fluid ounces
2 tablespoons	=	⅛ cup	=	1 ounce
4 tablespoons	=	¼ cup	=	2 ounces
16 tablespoons	=	1 cup	=	8 ounces
2 cups	=	1 pound	=	16 ounces

◆ METRIC CONVERSION ◆

1 milliliter	=	.034 fluid ounces
1 liter	=	33.8 fluid ounces or 4.2 cups
1 fluid ounce	=	29.56 milliliters
1 fluid cup	=	236 milliliters
1 fluid quart	=	946 milliliters or .946 liters
1 teaspoon	=	5 milliliters
1 tablespoon	=	15 milliliters

TWO

Fruit
and Vegetable
Basics

T his chapter contains some of the more important preserving information in this book. It includes such vital items as blanching charts, syrup tables, and freezing facts, as well as information on sugar alternatives in preserving and more. Read this chapter before you try any of the recipes for a basic understanding of the techniques used in microwave preserving.

Freezing fresh fruits in a sugar syrup allows great versatility and ease in menu planning. These fresh-flavored fruits with a sparkling of sweetness may be used for compotes, pies, cobblers, and ice cream toppings or served as is. Refer to the "Defrosting Frozen Fruit" chart if speed is of the essence.

If you are fortunate enough to have your own garden or access to fresh-picked vegetables, the microwave oven will be your best preserving friend. It is ideal for blanching fresh-picked vegetables. When blanching large quantities of vegetables, we recommend an assembly-line approach: Process one to two pounds at a time in the microwave oven while preparing the next batch. (See the Blanching Vegetables chart for complete details.) We find this method to be cool, easy, and efficient, and it produces superior, fresh-tasting vegetables.

TABLE 3

Defrosting Frozen Fruit

Amount	Defrosting Time at 30% Power *
10-ounce carton/container	3 to 4 minutes
1-pint container	5 to 6 minutes
1-quart container	9 to 10 minutes

* Let container rest for 5 to 10 minutes *after* microwaving to complete defrosting. Increase resting time for larger containers.

Fruit Freezing Facts

Most fruits freeze very well. If properly prepared they will retain their bright, natural colors, their flavors, and their nutritive value. Some guidelines to follow:

◆ Select fresh, ripe fruit, just as you would for eating.

◆ Wash the fruit gently in cold water; drain well.

◆ Decide on the method desired for freezing: in sugar syrup, unsweetened pack, or sugar pack.

◆ Prepare fruit for freezing and pack in appropriate freezer containers. Allow a ½-inch headspace for dry or sugar-packed fruits. Allow a 1-inch headspace for all liquid or syrup packs.

◆ Floating fruits that tend to darken can be kept below the surface of the liquid by crumpling waxed paper, parchment paper, or plastic wrap on top of the fruit in the container before sealing. These papers are not affected by microwave defrosting.

◆ Seal, label, and date containers. Freeze quickly at 0°F or below. Frozen fruits may be stored for 8 to 12 months. Do not refreeze thawed fruits.

TABLE 4

Frozen-Fruit Yield

To obtain 1 pint of frozen fruit, start with quantities
listed below:

Fruit	Amount
Apples	1¼ to 1½ pounds
Apricots	⅔ to ¾ pound
Berries, small *	1⅓ to 1½ pints
Berries, large **	1 pint
Cherries	1 pound
Peaches/Nectarines	1 to 1½ pounds
Pears	1 to 1¼ pounds
Rhubarb	⅔ to 1 pound
Strawberries	⅔ quart

* Such as blackberries, blueberries, elderberries, gooseberries,
and huckleberries.

** Such as boysenberries, loganberries, marionberries, and raspberries.

Freezing Fruit without Sugar

Some fruits, such as blueberries, don't require added sugar or
liquids for proper freezing. They are frozen in what is commonly
referred to as a "dry pack."

Other fruits, such as apples and peaches, will darken if not
treated before freezing. If you choose not to use sugar or sugar
syrup, you may substitute a solution of water and ascorbic-acid
color keeper, an ingredient commonly found in the grocery
store. Add ¾ teaspoon ascorbic-acid color keeper to each quart
of water. Place the prepared fruit in a freezer container. Pour

enough ascorbic acid–water solution over fruit to cover, leaving ½- to 1-inch headspace (varies with individual recipe). A good way to prevent floating fruit, which will darken, is to put crumpled wax, parchment, or other water-resistant paper in this headspace before sealing. Fruit prepared in this manner, often called a "wet pack," may be used later for microwave jams and jellies if desired, as well as in other recipes.

Sugar Syrups

Making sugar syrups in the microwave oven is a real shortcut when canning fruits. Use large glass measuring cups or a 2-quart microwave batter bowl to prepare sugar syrups. These will not only measure the ingredients but will also serve as excellent containers for microwave cooking. And they have pour spouts, which will make for easier filling of jars or freezer containers than the often-messy ladling method.

Type of Syrup	Sugar (cups)	Water (cups)	Minutes at HIGH (100% Power)	Yield (cups)
Light	1	4	12	5
Thin	2	4	13	5
Medium	3	4	14	5½
Heavy	4¾	4	16	6½
Very Heavy	7	4	18	7¾

In a two-quart batter bowl or large mixing bowl, combine the sugar and water in the amounts indicated above; stir to mix well. Microwave as directed until the mixture boils, stirring once halfway through the cooking time. Remove and stir, making sure the sugar is completely dissolved.

For canning: Pour hot sugar syrup into prepared jars full of fruit. If you need to keep the syrup hot until the jars are ready, hold the syrup on the oven's WARM (10% power) setting until needed. (If you have to keep it warm for more than sixty minutes, it may be simpler to reheat the syrup.)

For freezing: Let the syrup cool to room temperature, covered. Chill it in refrigerator. Be sure the syrup is well chilled before pouring it over the fruit in freezer containers.

To make ahead: Syrup may be made the day before and stored in the refrigerator.

To prevent darkened fruit: If sugar syrup is to be used on a fruit that tends to darken, add ¾ teaspoon ascorbic-acid color keeper to each quart of syrup after it has cooled to prevent darkening.

Alternatives to Canning with Sugar Syrups

You may wish to reduce the amount of sugar used or to eliminate it altogether. We have used the following substitutions successfully.

◆ Pack fruit in plain hot water. You may wish to add ascorbic acid to prevent darkening, if appropriate.

◆ Pack fruit in hot fruit juice. (Pineapple or pear juices are very sweet and are good choices if fruit is tart. You can also use the same type of juice as fruit being preserved.)

◆ Place one to two tablespoons of honey or pure maple syrup on top of fruit packed in jar and pour boiling water over before sealing jar for processing.

◆ For flavor enhancement, add one or more of the following to each jar of fruit: one slice of lemon, one clove, one cinnamon stick.

Process fruits conventionally in a boiling-water bath.

It's easy to use your microwave oven to heat water, fruit juices, or syrups quickly. Microwave on HIGH (100% power) until liquid reaches desired temperature or just until liquid comes to a boil. If heating syrup in a glass container, remember to remove lid first. Syrup at the narrow neck will be hotter than that in the rest of the bottle. Handle carefully; pot holders may be in order.

Selecting Vegetables for Freezing

The best vegetables for freezing probably come from your own garden.* However, fresh produce can also be found at roadside stands, U-pick farms, or even markets with excellent produce sections. Whatever your choice, select the freshest possible produce and prepare for freezing immediately or refrigerate until preparation time. Ideally, fresh vegetables should be gathered early in the morning before they have absorbed much heat. If you do have to store fresh vegetables, try to do so for the shortest time possible in order to obtain peak flavor, quality, and food value. Do not select overripe vegetables as they can be tough and flavorless.

   * Bell peppers, tomatoes, and potatoes, however, are not suitable for freezing.

What to Look for in a Vegetable

Asparagus
Young, tender, crisp stalks with well-formed, tightly closed tips; about 2-inch-long light-colored woody base.

Beans, green
Young, tender, with a crisp snap; long, straight pods.

Broccoli
Firm, tender (not woody) stalks; tight, compact, dark-green heads.

Brussels Sprouts
Firm, compact, small- to medium-sized, bright green heads.

Carrots
Firm, well-shaped, brightly colored, mild-flavored; not excessively large, woody, or shriveled.

Cauliflower
Firm, tender, heavy, compact, snow-white head with a bright green covering of leaves.

Celery
Firm, compact stalk, not pithy or stringy. Should be brittle enough to snap easily. Avoid stalks with brown spots or seed formation in center.

Corn
Young, tender, even rows of plump, milky kernels with a fresh green husk.

Onions, tiny white
Bright, clean, firm, and well shaped with dry skins. Avoid onions that have sprouted at the neck or have soft spots.

Parsnips
Firm, medium-sized, well-shaped, and smooth; avoid soft, very large, or limp parsnips.

Peas
Bright green, well-filled pods; plump peas.

Rutabagas
Firm, smooth, small to medium in size; heavy for size.

Snow Peas (or Sugar Snap Peas)
Bright green, slightly velvety, fresh-picked; avoid limp, discolored, wet, or mildewed pods.

Spinach
Young, tender leaves that are crisp, not limp.

Squash, summer
Young, with small seeds and firm, tender rind; heavy for size; glossy.

Squash, winter
Mature, fully colored, firm, hard rind; heavy for size.

Swiss Chard
Bright white or red stalks; young tender leaves that are crisp, not limp.

Turnips
Firm, smooth, fairly round; small to medium in size; heavy for size.

 To cut through the tough skins of a variety of winter squash (acorn, butternut, etc.) more easily, place whole squash in the microwave oven. Microwave on HIGH (100% power) for 1½ to 2½ minutes, depending upon size of the squash. Let stand for 2 minutes before cutting.

TABLE 5

Frozen-vegetable Yield

In general, the following amount of vegetable as purchased will yield one pint frozen:

Vegetable	Pounds
Asparagus	1 to 1½
Beans, green	⅔ to 1
Broccoli	1
Brussels Sprouts	1
Carrots, without tops	1¼ to 1½
Cauliflower	1⅓
Celery	1 to 1¼
Corn on the cob, in husks	2 to 2½
Onions, whole, tiny	1
Parsnips	1¼
Peas	2 to 2½
Snow Peas (or Sugar Snap Peas)	1
Spinach	1 to 1½
Squash, summer	1 to 1¼
Squash, winter	1½
Swiss Chard	1 to 1¼
Turnips	⅔

Cooking Frozen Vegetables in a Microwave Oven

There are basically two ways to cook frozen vegetables properly in a microwave oven. Vegetables frozen in heat-sealed plastic bags may be left in the bag for cooking, while vegetables frozen in rigid freezer containers must be removed and placed in a microwave-safe container for cooking. (*Note:* Do not use regular or freezer plastic bags to cook vegetables in the microwave oven. Even heavy-duty freezer bags will melt at low temperatures of 140 to 180°F.)

It is not necessary, with either method, to thaw or defrost vegetables or add large quantities of additional water. If water is added, a tablespoon or two is usually sufficient. Microwaved vegetables cook quickly (six to seven minutes per pound).

Cooking Vegetables in a Heat-sealed Plastic Bag

Place bag of frozen vegetables on microwave-safe plate or bowl. Cut a ½-inch slit on the top side of the bag.

For tender-crisp vegetables, microwave on HIGH (100% power) for 4 to 6 minutes. Quarter-turn dish halfway through cooking time if necessary. Let rest in container for 4 to 5 minutes. Check vegetables for desired doneness. Serve.

For softer, less crisp vegetables, microwave on HIGH for 5 to 8 minutes. (Cooking time will vary depending upon the type of vegetable being cooked; for example, petite peas take minimum time and lima beans take maximum time.) Quarter-turn dish halfway through cooking time if necessary. Let rest in container 5 to 10 minutes. Check vegetables for desired doneness before serving.

Blanching Vegetables

Prepare vegetable as indicated below. Place vegetable in microwave container; cover with lid or plastic wrap. Microwave on HIGH (100% power) for all blanching times shown. After blanching, drain vegetable in colander. Plunge colander containing vegetable into ice water for several minutes. Drain; then pack in freezer container, seal, label, date, and freeze.

Asparagus
2 cups (1 pound). Wash. Trim off white woody ends. Cut to container length or 2-inch pieces. For long stalks, alternate top and bottom ends when placing in blanching container. Add ¼ cup water; cover. Rearrange or stir halfway through cooking. Chill, pack, and freeze. Blanching time: 3 minutes.

Green Beans
3 cups (1 pound). Wash. Remove ends. Cut into 1- or 2-inch pieces. (For French-cut green beans, cut each bean lengthwise into 4 or more strips.) Add ½ cup water; cover. Stir halfway through cooking. Chill, pack, and freeze. Blanching time: 4 minutes.

Broccoli
3 cups (1½ pounds). Wash. Trim base stalk; peel large end of stalk if desired. Split lengthwise into 1-inch stalks. For chopped broccoli, cut into ½-inch pieces after trimming. Add ½ cup water; cover. Rearrange or stir halfway through cooking. Chill, pack, and freeze. Blanching time: 5 minutes.

Brussels Sprouts
4 cups (1 pound). Cut from stem; wash well. Remove imperfect outer leaves. (*Note:* If precut from stem at purchase, trim base.) Add ¼ cup water; cover. Stir once halfway through cooking. Chill, pack, and freeze. Blanching time: 4½ minutes.

Carrots
4 cups (1¼ pounds). Wash; scrape or peel. Cut into ¼-inch slices. Add ½ cup water; cover. Stir once halfway through cooking. Chill, pack, and freeze. Blanching time: 5 minutes.

Cauliflower
1 head (1 pound). Wash. Trim woody base and cut into small florets or 1-inch pieces. Add ½ cup water; cover. Stir halfway through cooking. Chill, pack, and freeze. Blanching time: 3½ minutes.

Celery
4 cups (1 pound). Wash. Trim base and leafy tops. Cut into ½-inch slices (tops optional). Add ⅛ cup water; cover. Stir once halfway through cooking. Chill, pack, and freeze. Blanching time: 6 minutes.

Corn, kernel
2 cups. Husk; remove silk and wash. Cut corn kernels off (whole or cream style) and place in blanching container. Add ⅛ cup water; cover. Stir once halfway through cooking. Chill, pack, and freeze. Blanching time: 3 minutes.

Corn, on the cob (in husk)
4 ears (may be prepared and frozen in husk). Trim both ends of excess silk and stem. Remove excessive outer husk. Rinse and shake to dry partly. *(Note:* For long-term (more than 3 months) freezer storage, we recommend removing corn kernels from cob before blanching as above.) Arrange ears with 1 inch of air space on all sides. Rearrange halfway through cooking. Chill, pack, and freeze. Blanching time: 4 minutes.

Corn, on the cob (out of husk)
4 ears. Husk; remove silk, wash, and trim off excess stem. Add ¼ cup water; cover. Rearrange halfway through cooking. Chill, pack, and freeze. Blanching time: 4½ minutes.

Onions, chopped
4½ cups (1¼ pounds). Trim both ends; slit outer skin from top to bottom. Peel away outer layer. Rinse; chop. Add ¼ cup water; cover. Stir halfway through cooking. Chill, pack, and freeze. Blanching time: 3½ minutes.

Onions, whole, tiny
2 cups (¾ pound). Trim both ends; slit outer skin from top to bottom. Peel off outer layer; rinse. Add ¼ cup water; cover. Stir halfway through cooking. Chill, pack, and freeze. Blanching time: 3 minutes.

Parsnips
Scant 2 cups (⅔ pound). Wash and peel. Trim ends and cut into ½-inch cubes. Add ¼ cup water; cover. Stir halfway through cooking. Chill, pack, and freeze. Blanching time: 3 minutes.

Peas
2 cups (2 pounds). Shell; discard imperfect peas. Add ¼ cup water; cover. Stir halfway through cooking. Chill, pack, and freeze. Blanching time: 3½ minutes.

Rutabagas
4 cups (1¼ pounds). Wash; cut off tops, peel, and cut into ½-inch cubes. Add ½ cup water; cover. Stir halfway through cooking. Chill, pack, and freeze. Blanching time: 5 minutes.

Snow Peas (or Sugar Snap Peas)
2 cups (1 pound). Snap off ends and remove strings. Rinse. Add ⅛ cup water; cover. Stir halfway through cooking. Chill, pack, and freeze. Blanching time: 2 minutes.

Spinach
12 cups (1 pound). Wash well; soak in cold water for 5 minutes. Rinse with cold water. Cut and discard thick stem ends and any imperfect leaves. Add ⅛ cup water; cover. Stir halfway through cooking. Chill, pack, and freeze. Blanching time: 3 to 3½ minutes.

Squash, summer (all varieties)
(1 pound). Wash; trim both ends. Cut into ½-inch slices or chunks. Add ¼ cup water; cover. Stir halfway through cooking. Chill, pack, and freeze. Blanching time: 2½ to 4 minutes.

Swiss Chard
10 cups (1 pound). Wash well. Trim any imperfect leaves and stem ends. Cut into 1-inch pieces. Add ⅛ cup water; cover. Stir halfway through cooking. Chill, pack, and freeze. Blanching time: 3 to 3½ minutes.

Turnips
3 cups (¾ pound). Wash; cut off tops, peel, and cut into ½-inch cubes. Add ¼ cup water; cover. Stir halfway through cooking. Chill, pack, and freeze. Blanching time: 3 minutes.

Rehydrating Dried Vegetables

To rehydrate dried vegetables easily, place them in a microwave-safe bowl. Pour cold water over the vegetables and stir once gently to make sure the vegetables are immersed in water. Cover bowl with a microwave-safe cover or plastic wrap. Microwave on HIGH (100% power) just to the boiling point. Remove bowl from oven. Leave cover in place, set aside, and let rest until vegetables are completely rehydrated.

Basic Spaghetti Sauce

Capture the special flavor of fresh summer tomatoes with this easy and popular recipe. Makes about 2 quarts.

4 cups (32 ounces) Freezer-fresh Stewed Tomatoes*
2 cups (16 ounces) tomato sauce
1 6-ounce can tomato paste
1 cup sliced mushrooms
½ cup green bell pepper, seeded and chopped
½ cup red wine
1 tablespoon sugar (optional)
1 tablespoon fresh *or* 1 teaspoon dried basil
1 tablespoon fresh *or* 1 teaspoon dried parsley
1 teaspoon fresh or dried thyme
1 teaspoon fresh or dried marjoram
1 teaspoon fresh or dried oregano
1 teaspoon minced garlic (optional)
¼ teaspoon pepper
Salt to taste

Combine all ingredients in a 4-quart or larger microwave-safe mixing bowl; stir well. Cover with plastic wrap. Microwave on HIGH (100% power) for 7 minutes, or until mixture comes to a boil. Stir halfway through cooking time. Remove cover and stir again. Microwave on MEDIUM (50% power) for 20 minutes, stirring every 5 minutes. Cool and pack in freezer containers, leaving a ½-inch headspace.

Variation

Spaghetti Sauce with Meat or Meat Substitute. Sauté 1 pound lean ground beef, veal, or Italian sausage or prepare equivalent meat substitute. Drain and combine with the ingredients at the beginning of the recipe.

    * If substituting canned stewed tomatoes, add ½ cup sautéed chopped onion to this recipe.

If using plastic wrap to make a cover for a bowl, be sure to leave a "vent" (a small lifted corner) or prick the top with a toothpick to allow steam to escape. Always lift plastic wrap away from you carefully to avoid hot steam, which can burn.

Lentil Spaghetti Sauce

An excellent vegetarian spaghetti sauce. Makes about 3 cups.

1 cup water
¼ cup lentils
½ onion, chopped
½ bell pepper, seeded and chopped
1 to 2 garlic cloves, minced
1 teaspoon olive oil
2 cups *or* 1 15-ounce can tomato sauce
1 cup chopped tomatoes
1 teaspoon Italian seasoning
¼ teaspoon sugar (optional)
½ teaspoon ground black pepper

In a 2-cup glass measure combine water and lentils; stir. Microwave on HIGH (100% power) for 2½ minutes, or until water comes to a boil. Set aside.

In a 3- to 4-quart microwave-safe mixing bowl combine onion, pepper, garlic, and oil. Sauté in microwave on HIGH for 3½ to 4 minutes, or until onion is translucent, stirring once or twice. Combine remaining ingredients and microwave on HIGH for 10 minutes, or until mixture comes to a boil, stirring once halfway through. Lower power to MEDIUM (50%) and microwave for 10 minutes, stirring every 4 to 5 minutes. Cool. Use immediately or ladle into clean freezer containers, leaving a 1-inch headspace. Seal and freeze.

Easy Marinara Sauce

The summer-fresh taste of this classic sauce can be captured for year-round enjoyment with a little help from your microwave oven and freezer. Use this sauce in lasagne, manicotti, spaghetti, and other Italian dishes. Makes about 1 quart.

1 teaspoon olive oil
⅓ cup finely chopped onion *or* 1 tablespoon minced dried onion
2 to 3 garlic cloves, peeled and minced
4 cups *or* 2 15-ounce cans tomato sauce
3 tablespoons minced fresh parsley *or* 2 tablespoons dried parsley
1 tablespoon chopped basil
1 teaspoon oregano (fresh or dried)
1 teaspoon granulated sugar
½ teaspoon ground black pepper
Salt to taste

Combine oil, onion, and garlic in a large microwave-safe bowl. Microwave on HIGH (100% power) for 2½ minutes, stirring once. Add all remaining ingredients and microwave on HIGH for 10 minutes, or until mixture comes to a boil, stirring halfway through. Stir and lower power to MEDIUM (50%); microwave for 8 to 10 minutes, stirring halfway through. Use immediately or cool and ladle into clean freezer containers, leaving a 1-inch headspace. Seal and freeze.

Variations

Chunky Marinara Sauce. After cooking onion and garlic, add 3 coarsely chopped, fresh peeled tomatoes. Cook as directed. You may have to increase cooking time by 1 to 2 minutes.

Vegetable or Meat Marinara Sauce. After cooking onion and garlic, add some or all of the following: sautéed mushrooms, bell peppers, shallots, meat, or sausage. Cook as directed.

To cook foods as quickly as possible in your microwave oven, be sure to keep your oven cavity clean. Food splatters will divert microwaves from what you wish to cook, and this will add to overall cooking time.

A good cleaning solution for your microwave oven consists of 2 tablespoons vinegar to 2 cups water. Put it in a pint spray bottle and keep it handy for spills.

Pizza Sauce

For maximum convenience, keep this on hand in the freezer in portion sizes that can be quickly thawed on your microwave oven's defrost cycle. Makes about 2 half-pint portions.

2 cups (16 ounces) tomato sauce
1 6-ounce can tomato paste
1 garlic clove, minced (optional)
1 bay leaf (optional)
1 tablespoon sugar
1 teaspoon Worcestershire sauce
½ teaspoon Italian seasoning
½ teaspoon salt, or to taste (optional)
¼ teaspoon ground black pepper

Combine all ingredients in a 2-quart microwave-safe bowl; mix thoroughly. Microwave on HIGH (100% power) for 4 minutes, or until mixture just begins to come to a boil. Stir and reduce power to MEDIUM-HIGH (70%); microwave for 6 minutes, stirring once halfway through. Remove bay leaf. Pour into sterile jars or freezer containers. Refrigerate for short-term use or freeze for longer storage.

Basic Freezer Tomato Sauce

Fresh garden herbs are wonderful in this recipe. You can vary the herbs used to suit individual tastes or recipes. Makes 2 1/2 pints.

8 cups ripe tomatoes, peeled* and quartered (about 4 1/2 pounds)
2 tablespoons finely chopped fresh or dried parsley
1 tablespoon granulated sugar (optional)
1 tablespoon fresh *or* 1 teaspoon dried basil
1/2 teaspoon fresh or dried oregano
1/4 teaspoon fresh or dried thyme
1/4 teaspoon fresh or dried rosemary
1 bay leaf
Salt and pepper to taste

Process tomatoes in food processor or blender until pureed.* Place tomato puree in a 4-quart or larger microwave-safe bowl. Add remaining ingredients and stir to combine. Cover with plastic wrap and microwave on HIGH (100% power) for 8 minutes, or until mixture comes to a boil. Stir and reduce power to MEDIUM-HIGH (70%); microwave for 30 to 35 minutes, or until mixture reaches a slightly thickened consistency, stirring every 5 minutes. Remove bay leaf and allow to cool. Ladle into freezer containers, leaving a 1/2-inch headspace. Freeze.

Variations

Chunky Tomato Sauce. Peel 2 additional tomatoes and coarsely chop. Add to sauce during the last 10 minutes of cooking time. Proceed as directed.

Mushroom Sauce. Place 1 cup sliced mushrooms and 1 teaspoon butter, margarine, or olive oil in a microwave-safe bowl. Microwave on HIGH for 3 minutes, stirring halfway through. Add to sauce during last 5 minutes of cooking time. Proceed as directed.

Green Pepper and Onion Sauce. Cut 1 small to medium bell pepper and 1 small onion into chunks. Place onion and pepper and 2 teaspoons butter, margarine, or olive oil in a microwave-safe bowl; microwave on HIGH for 3 to 4 minutes, or until onion is slightly translucent. Add to sauce during the last 10 minutes of cooking. Proceed as directed.

*A food mill may be used instead of a food processor or blender. Quarter, but do not peel, tomatoes for food mill. Proceed as directed.

Freezer-fresh Stewed Tomatoes

A good basic recipe that is perfect to make up as your garden tomatoes ripen. Makes about 3 pints.

3 pounds fresh tomatoes (about 6 cups chopped)
1 large celery stalk, chopped
¼ to ½ large onion, or to taste, chopped
½ teaspoon salt, or to taste (optional)

Peel tomatoes (see Micro-Tip, page 90), remove stem ends, and chop coarsely.

Place all vegetables in a 4-quart or larger microwave-safe mixing bowl; add salt and stir to combine. Cover with plastic wrap or lid, leaving a vent in plastic wrap. Microwave on HIGH (100% power) for 5 minutes, or until mixture comes to a boil. Remove cover, stir, and microwave on MEDIUM-HIGH (70% power) for 3 minutes. Cool and ladle into freezer containers, leaving a ½-inch headspace. Freeze.

Cream of Vegetable Soup

Warm, hearty, and full of vegetable goodness. Makes about 5 cups.

Base:
1 tablespoon butter or margarine
½ cup chopped onion
1 celery stalk, sliced
2 cups chopped broccoli or cauliflower
1 medium carrot, shredded or grated
1½ cups hot chicken or vegetable broth

To serve:
1 cup evaporated milk
1 teaspoon lemon juice
½ to 1 teaspoon salt
¼ teaspoon white pepper
½ teaspoon (or more) herb of choice (e.g., basil, chervil, marjoram, parsley, rosemary, thyme)

In a 3- to 4-quart or larger microwave-safe bowl, combine butter, onion, and celery. Microwave on HIGH (100% power) for 2 minutes, or until onion is soft and translucent. Stir halfway through cooking time. Add broccoli and carrot, stirring to mix. Cover with plastic wrap, leaving vent. Microwave on HIGH for 6 to 7 minutes, or until vegetables are tender. Pour in ½ cup hot broth; stir. Puree vegetables in blender or food processor if desired. Add remaining hot broth. Base can be refrigerated at this point or frozen for longer storage.

When ready to serve, add remaining ingredients to thawed base, stirring to combine. Microwave 8 to 10 minutes on HIGH. *Do not boil.* Taste and adjust seasonings. Serve.

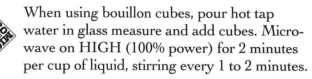 When using bouillon cubes, pour hot tap water in glass measure and add cubes. Microwave on HIGH (100% power) for 2 minutes per cup of liquid, stirring every 1 to 2 minutes.

Fruits and
Fruit Sauces

THREE

Thinking chapter is a potpourri of fruits and fruit sauces, all so
simple to make in your microwave oven. We have found that
fruits are an absolute natural in the microwave: Because of their
delicate nature, they require little cooking. You'll find family
favorites such as Chunky Applesauce and Basic Cranberry
Sauce as well as such unique gourmet delights as Zucchini
Applesauce and Wild Blackberry Topping with Liqueur.

One question we are often asked is, "Can you dry fruit
leathers in a microwave oven?" The answer is, "Not well." The
microwave oven is a moist-cooking appliance and, as such, it
doesn't dry exceptionally well.

Drying fruit leathers is best done in a food dryer, especially
where large quantities are desired. The microwave oven can,
however, assist in this process by quickly and easily preheating
and precooking the pureed fruit. This eliminates the browning
that occurs with some fruits. It also makes the use of preserva-
tives unnecessary and will speed up the drying process.

Microwave and Food-dryer Preparation of Fruit Leather

This method works especially well with apricots, apples,
peaches, and pears but can be used with most fruits and berries.
Quantity: 2½ cups fruit puree makes one 18" x 14" x ⅛" sheet of
fruit leather.

Pureed fruit of choice

Place pureed fruit in 2-quart microwave-safe batter bowl or
larger mixing bowl, as appropriate to quantity. Cover with plas-

tic wrap and microwave on HIGH (100% power) 4 to 5 minutes. Stir occasionally. (Stop when tiny bubbles appear around the edges of the bowl.) Do not let boil.

Pour heated puree onto food-dryer trays designed for fruit leathers. Dry in food dryer at 130 to 135°F until done (about 8 hours).

Chunky Applesauce

A versatile recipe; the apples can be coarsely chopped, finely chopped, or blended to produce the texture preferred. Makes about 3 pints.

6 cups peeled, seeded, and coarsely chunked or chopped apples (about 8 apples)
¼ cup water
½ to 1 teaspoon ground cinnamon (optional)
½ to ¾ cup granulated sugar

In a deep 3-quart or larger bowl combine apples, water, and cinnamon. Cover bowl with plastic wrap, lifting one corner up for a steam vent. Microwave on HIGH (100% power) for 4 minutes. Stir, recover, and microwave on HIGH power for 4 minutes more. Stir in sugar. Microwave for 2 minutes on HIGH. Let stand, covered, for 5 to 10 minutes. Place in containers.
For immediate use: Refrigerate up to 2 weeks.
For longer storage: Freeze, leaving a 1-inch headspace.
To can: Pack into jars while hot. Process sealed jars conventionally in a boiling-water-bath canner for 15 minutes.

Variations

Traditional Applesauce. Cook as directed. Stir and mash cooked apples to desired consistency. A food processor or blender may be used.

Chunky Pearsauce. Substitute pears for apples, omitting water. Cook and store as directed for applesauce.

Smooth Pearsauce. Follow directions for Traditional Applesauce.

Zucchini Applesauce

Tastes just like applesauce. What a sneaky way to use up that excess zucchini! Makes 2½ cups.

¼ cup water
¼ teaspoon salt (optional)
2 whole cloves
2 thin lemon slices
2 cups peeled and chopped zucchini (about 2 medium)
2 cups peeled, cored, and chopped apples (about 2 large apples)
½ cup granulated sugar
½ teaspoon ground cinnamon
1 tablespoon lemon juice

In a large microwave-safe mixing bowl combine water, salt, cloves, and lemon slices. Stir and microwave on HIGH (100% power) for 1 minute or until mixture comes to a boil. Stir in zucchini and apples. Cover bowl with plastic wrap and microwave on HIGH for 6 minutes, or until tender, stirring once halfway through cooking. Remove cloves and lemon slices. Pour into blender or food processor and process until desired texture is reached (this goes very quickly).

Pour back into mixing bowl and stir in sugar, cinnamon, and lemon juice. Pour into container(s). Serve at room temperature or chilled.

For immediate use: Refrigerate up to 2 weeks.

For longer storage: Freeze, leaving a 1-inch headspace.

Basic Cranberry Sauce

Microwave cranberry sauce is amazingly easy to make and delightfully fresh-tasting. Makes 1 quart.

1 pound fresh or frozen cranberries (about 3½ cups)
1 cup sugar
⅓ cup water

In a 3-quart microwave-safe bowl or casserole, combine all ingredients; mix well. Microwave, covered, on HIGH (100% power) for 6 minutes, stirring once halfway through cooking time. Check for doneness; cranberry skins should have popped. If they have not, continue cooking for 1 to 2 minutes. Let rest, covered, for 10 minutes.

For immediate use: Refrigerate up to 3 to 4 weeks. For longer storage: Pack and freeze, leaving a ½-inch headspace in container.

Variation

Cranberry-Orange Sauce. Substitute orange juice for water and add 1 tablespoon fresh grated orange peel. Optional: Add ¼ cup chopped walnuts after cooking.

 Using hot tap water in recipes calling for water can shorten the microwave cooking time.

Cranberry Jewels in Liqueur

This elegant and colorful sauce is perfect for special meals and makes a lovely gift. The recipe is from Classic Fruit Liqueurs *by Cheryl Long and Heather Kibbey. Makes about 3 cups.*

2 cups cranberries, fresh or frozen
1 cup sugar
½ cup orange juice
¼ cup orange liqueur
1 11-ounce can Mandarin oranges, well drained

In a 1½ to 2-quart microwave-safe casserole or bowl, combine cranberries, sugar, and orange juice. Cover and microwave on HIGH (100% power) for 3 minutes. Stir and microwave for 2 to 3 minutes more, or until cranberries have popped their skins. Let stand, covered, for 5 minutes. Gently stir in liqueur and drained Mandarin orange sections. Refrigerate, covered, overnight before serving. Keeps in the refrigerator for 1 week.

Rhubarb Sauce

This versatile sauce makes a quick fruit dish topped with cream. It is also an excellent cobbler base. Makes 1 quart.

4 cups sliced fresh rhubarb stalks *
3 tablespoons water
1 cup sugar

In a 3-quart microwave-safe bowl, combine rhubarb and water; cover. Microwave on HIGH (100% power) for 6 minutes, stirring once halfway through cooking time. Stir in sugar and microwave, covered, 1½ minutes more on HIGH to dissolve sugar; stir again. Cool. Serve warm or chilled.

For immediate use: Place in covered container and refrigerate up to 1 week.

For longer storage: Pack in freezer containers, leaving a 1-inch headspace; freeze.

To can: Pour hot sauce into hot, sterile jars, leaving a ½-inch headspace. Seal and process in a conventional boiling-water-bath canner for 15 minutes (half-pints or pints).

    * Frozen rhubarb may be substituted for fresh in this recipe; if it is, omit the water.

Sweet-and-Sour Sauce

Make your own sweet-and-sour sauce easily and economically in your microwave oven. This is a perfect make-ahead recipe that stores well in the refrigerator. Fresh pineapple may be substituted. Makes about 1 pint.

⅓ cup chopped onion
⅓ cup green bell pepper chunks
½ teaspoon butter or margarine
⅔ cup sugar
2 tablespoons soy sauce
¼ cup white or cider vinegar
¼ cup catsup
2 tablespoons cornstarch
½ cup pineapple juice, reserved from canned pineapple *
½ cup pineapple tidbits, drained

Place onion, green pepper, and butter in a 1-cup glass measure. Cover with plastic wrap and microwave on HIGH (100% power) for 1½ minutes; set aside.

    Combine sugar, soy sauce, vinegar, and catsup in a 2- to 3-quart microwave-safe bowl; stir to combine. Microwave on HIGH for 1½ to 2 minutes, or until mixture comes to a boil, stirring after 1 minute. Mix cornstarch and pineapple juice until smooth and whisk into sauce. Microwave on HIGH for 3 minutes, stirring every minute, until sauce is thickened and clear. Stir in onion, green pepper, and pineapple. Serve immediately or refrigerate and reheat when ready to serve.

    *If short on juice, add water to make ½ cup.

Easy Berry Sauce

Whip up this quick and easy sauce using blackberries, blueberries, raspberries, or strawberries. Serve over ice cream or pound cake, or use to make a plain cheesecake spectacular. Makes about 1 pint.

2⅓ cups fresh or frozen berries
⅓ cup granulated sugar or honey or pure maple syrup
1 tablespoon cornstarch
¼ cup water (omit if using honey or maple syrup)
1 tablespoon lemon juice
2 tablespoons lemon, orange, or blueberry liqueur (optional)

Mash ⅓ cup berries with fork; set remaining berries aside. Combine mashed berries with remaining ingredients, except reserved berries, in a 4-cup or larger glass measure. Microwave on HIGH (100% power) for 1 minute; stir. Microwave on HIGH for 1 to 2 minutes more, or until thickened. Stir in reserved berries. Chill until ready to serve. Will keep in refrigerator for several days.

Raspberry Dessert Sauce

This sauce is a natural. It's fresh-tasting, colorful, low in sugar, and it makes a plain dessert look spectacular. Try it over cheesecake or pound cake. Create "designer" desserts by pouring the sauce onto a dessert plate and arranging fruits, meringue, ice cream, etc. on top. Use your imagination! Makes about 3 cups.

1¼ pounds fresh raspberries *or* 2 10-ounce packages frozen unsweetened raspberries, thawed
¼ to ⅓ cup granulated sugar, to taste
1 tablespoon Kirsch

Wash fresh berries in cool water; drain well. Push berries through a fine sieve placed over a medium microwave-safe mixing bowl. Discard berry pulp. Add sugar to raspberry juice. Microwave on HIGH (100% power) for 2 to 3 minutes, stirring once halfway through. Remove and stir again, making sure sugar is well dissolved. Stir in Kirsch. Let cool and refrigerate. Serve chilled.

For immediate use: Let cool and refrigerate. This will keep for several days.

For longer storage: Prepare as directed but do not add Kirsch. Pour into freezer container(s) when cooled slightly, leaving a ½-inch headspace. Cover, label, and freeze. When ready to use, defrost in microwave on DEFROST (30% power) until liquid but not hot; stir in Kirsch. Serve or refrigerate for serving later.

Wild Blackberry Topping with Liqueur

This elegant sauce is surprisingly easy to make. It is a superb topping for ice cream, pound cake, or cheesecake and can also be layered in a trifle. What a perfect liqueur-lover's gift! Makes 3 half-pint jars.

4 cups blackberries, washed and drained
2 cups granulated sugar
¼ cup lemon or orange liqueur

Place washed berries in a 3-quart or larger microwave-safe bowl. Crush slightly. Microwave on HIGH (100% power) for 5 minutes. Stir in sugar and microwave on MEDIUM-HIGH (70%) power for 20 minutes, stirring every 5 minutes. Remove from microwave oven and let cool for 5 minutes; stir in liqueur. Ladle into sterile jars, seal, and label.

For immediate use: Place in covered container and refrigerate up to 3 weeks.

To can: Ladle into hot, sterile jars, leaving a ½-inch headspace. Seal and process conventionally in a boiling-water-bath canner for 5 minutes.

Chocolate-dipped Dried Fruit

Make these elegant and delicious chocolate-dipped fruits for special occasions or give them as gifts. While a wide variety of dried fruits may be used, our favorites are apricots, pears, and prunes. Makes about 3 to 4 dozen.

1 4-ounce bar German sweet chocolate or semisweet chocolate
2 tablespoons whipping cream
3 to 4 dozen pieces dried fruit of choice

In a 1-quart microwave-safe bowl, break chocolate into pieces. Add cream. Microwave on MEDIUM-HIGH (70% power) for 1 minute; stir and continue to microwave on same power for 30 seconds more, or until chocolate is melted when stirred.

Dip ⅓ to ½ of 1 piece of fruit in chocolate. Place on waxed paper to cool. Repeat with remaining fruit. Refrigerate until chocolate sets. Store in covered container in refrigerator.

Variation

Chocolate-dipped Fresh Fruit. Substitute fresh fruit, such as strawberries or cherries, for dried fruit. Follow directions for dried fruit. Chill and serve immediately.

 PLUMPING DRIED FRUITS

For moist and plump dried fruits, place dried fruits in a glass measuring cup or bowl and cover with warm tap water or other liquid.* Microwave on HIGH (100% power) just until liquid comes to a boil. One cup each of dried fruits and water will take about 3 to 4 minutes. Let rest 5 to 10 minutes.

* You can substitute fruit juice, wine, rum, sherry brandy, or liqueurs for the water to create unique and tasty variations for special cakes, fruitcakes, puddings, etc.

Spiced Crab Apples

Old-fashioned spiced crab apples are easy to make in your microwave oven. They're extra-special served with roast pork. Makes about 5 pints.

2½ pounds crab apples
3 cups granulated sugar
1 cup white or cider vinegar
1 cup water
2 cinnamon sticks, broken in half *
1 teaspoon whole cloves
6 to 8 drops red food coloring (optional)

Rinse crab apples; remove and discard stems. Set apples aside.

In a deep 4-quart or larger glass bowl, combine sugar, vinegar, water, and spices. Stir to mix well. Microwave on HIGH (100% power) for 10 to 12 minutes, or until mixture comes to a boil, stirring once halfway through cooking time. Add crab apples, stirring gently, and microwave on HIGH until mixture just returns to a boil. Reduce to MEDIUM (50% power) and microwave for about 10 to 12 minutes, or until crab apples are tender. Stir gently from time to time.

Remove bowl from microwave oven. Use a slotted spoon to remove crab apples from syrup and loosely pack apples in hot, sterile pint jars, leaving a ½-inch headspace. (Do not overpack apples or they will lose their shape.) Return bowl with syrup to microwave oven and bring back to a boil on HIGH (usually 2 minutes). Remove bowl from oven and stir in food coloring, if desired. Pour syrup over apples up to ½-inch headspace. Wipe rims and seal. Process sealed jars conventionally in a boiling-water-bath canner for 20 minutes; start timing when water comes to a boil.

* Do not use ground cinnamon as it can cause syrup to boil over.

Use the two- and three-step "memory" on your microwave oven to help you remember when to stir. For example, if a recipe calls for 10 minutes of microwave cooking, stirring once halfway through, do the following: Set oven on HIGH (100% power) for 5 minutes on the first memory, then set on HIGH for 5 minutes on the second memory. When the timer rings after the first 5 minutes, it will remind you to stir.

Spiced Prunes

Spiced prunes are excellent for breakfast or brunch. They are a fast and easy make-ahead dish, and they keep well in the refrigerator. Makes about 1 quart.

2 cups pitted dried prunes
2 cups hot tap water
¼ cup packed brown sugar or honey
1 to 2 cinnamon sticks
3 whole cloves
6 whole allspice berries
¼ teaspoon grated lemon rind

Combine all ingredients in a 2-quart microwave-safe casserole or batter bowl. Stir gently and cover with lid or plastic wrap. Microwave on HIGH (100% power) for 4 to 5 minutes, or until mixture just comes to a boil. Let cool and refrigerate, covered, overnight for best flavor. Remove spices before serving.

Variations

Spiced Fruit Compote. Substitute 1½ cups mixed dried fruits of your choice for that amount of prunes and prepare as directed.
Port Fruit Compote. Add ½ cup port just before serving.

Frozen Melon-Ball Mix

Freezer-fresh melon balls can be frozen and enjoyed all year long. Serve for breakfast, brunch, appetizer, or dessert. Serve partially thawed, as is, or with a little ginger ale poured over. Makes about 6 pints.

2 cups granulated sugar

4 cups water

½ cup lemonade concentrate

½ cup orange juice concentrate

8 cups assorted melon balls (Persian, watermelon, cantaloupe, honeydew, casaba, etc.)

1 cup blueberries

In a 2-quart microwave-safe batter bowl, combine sugar and water; stir. Microwave on HIGH (100% power) for 6 to 8 minutes, or until mixture comes to a boil, stirring twice. Remove and stir, making sure sugar is completely dissolved. Add lemonade and orange juice concentrates to hot sugar syrup, mixing well. Let cool while packing fruit into freezer containers. Pour cooled syrup over melon balls, leaving a ½-inch headspace. Seal and freeze.

TIP Covering a bowl with a lid or plastic wrap will help bring food to a boil faster.

Dried Citrus Peel

Fresh-tasting dried citrus peel is quick, easy, and economical to make in your microwave oven.

1 orange *or*
2 lemons *or*
3 limes

Finely grate peel onto a square of waxed paper. Spread peel evenly over waxed paper. Microwave on HIGH (100% power) for 2 to 2½ minutes. Stir to rearrange peel every minute. Let cool. Test for dryness. Place dried peel in an airtight container. Store at room temperature indefinitely or freeze for longer storage.

Old-fashioned Brandied Fruit

This recipe updates an old, time-consuming favorite. Apricots, cherries, seedless grapes, kumquats, peaches, pineapple, or plums may be used singly or in any combination you desire. Serve over ice cream, pound cake, cheesecake, or any other dessert your imagination can envision. Also excellent with ham. Makes about 3 pints.

1½ cups granulated sugar
½ cup water
3½ pounds firm, ripe fruit
¾ cup brandy

Prepare fruit: Wash, pit, cut, destem, etc., as appropriate. Treat fruit to prevent darkening, if desired (see page 12). Let fruit drain; set aside.

Combine sugar and water in a 4-cup or larger glass measure. Stir and microwave on HIGH (100% power) for 2 minutes, or until mixture comes to a boil. Stir and microwave on HIGH 1 to 2 minutes longer, or until all sugar is dissolved. Keep sugar syrup hot on lowest microwave power setting.

Pack drained fruit in hot, sterilized jars, leaving a 1-inch headspace. Add brandy to reserved sugar syrup, stirring to combine. Divide syrup evenly between jars, leaving a ½-inch headspace. Seal. Let cool and store.

For immediate use: Refrigerate for 1 month or more.

For longer storage: Process sealed jars conventionally in a boiling-water bath for 20 minutes. Cool and store.

Pickled Cherries

Any variety of sweet cherries may be used in this recipe. Pickled cherries are excellent with pork, ham, or pâtés, and they keep extremely well in the refrigerator. Makes about 2 pints.

1¼ pounds fresh sweet cherries, stems removed
½ cup sugar
2 cups red- or white-wine vinegar
2 cinnamon sticks

Wash cherries and pat dry. Pack in sterilized jars. In a 3- to 4-quart microwave-safe bowl, place sugar, vinegar, and cinnamon sticks; stir to combine. Microwave on HIGH (100% power) for 4 to 5 minutes, or until mixture comes to a boil, stirring once halfway through cooking time. Stir to check that sugar has dissolved. If not, cook until dissolved. Place one cinnamon stick in each jar. Pour hot syrup over cherries and seal. Cool and refrigerate until needed.

Mincemeat

An old-fashioned mincemeat in taste, but without the unhealthy fat. Our taste-testers loved this one, and we bet you will too. Makes about 3 pints.

8 cups peeled, cored, and chunked apple (about 8 apples)
2 cups raisins
½ cup chopped dates
2½ to 3 cups packed brown sugar
½ cup cider vinegar
1 teaspoon orange zest
1 teaspoon lemon zest
1 teaspoon ground cinnamon
½ teaspoon ground cloves
½ teaspoon ground mace
¼ teaspoon ground allspice
¼ teaspoon ground nutmeg
½ to 1 teaspoon salt
2 tablespoons sherry or brandy (optional)

Grind or finely chop apple chunks. Place ground apples in a 4-quart or larger microwave-safe bowl. Add all remaining ingredients except sherry. Stir to mix well. Microwave on HIGH (100% power) for 13 to 14 minutes, or until mixture just reaches a boil, stirring every 3 to 4 minutes. Reduce power to MEDIUM (50%); stir and continue cooking for 25 minutes, stirring every 6 to 7 minutes. Remove from microwave oven and stir in sherry, if desired. Pack in hot sterile jars; seal.

For immediate use: Serve immediately or refrigerate in covered container until ready to use (will keep for 1 to 2 weeks).

For longer storage: Ladle into freezer containers, leaving a ½-inch headspace. Seal, label, and freeze.

Variations

Green Tomato Mincemeat. Substitute peeled, chopped green tomatoes for half of the apples. Proceed as directed.

Citron or Currant Mincemeat. Substitute ½ to 1 cup citron or currants for the same amount of raisins. Proceed as directed.

FOUR

Jams, Jellies, and More

$\mathbf{M}$icrowave jam and jelly making is our favorite preserving technique. It allows small-batch preparation, which fits into our busy schedules. In addition, we know our preserves won't scorch and won't require constant attention. Boil-overs are a thing of the past as long as a large, deep bowl is used. Be sure to read our "Jam And Jelly Tips" before making your first batch.

Either liquid or powdered pectin may be used in microwave jam and jelly making. It is best, however, not to substitute one for another in a given recipe. The key to understanding the use of these two pectins is to remember that powdered pectin is boiled with the fruit so that it dissolves before the sugar is added, while liquid pectin is already dissolved and can be added with the sugar.

We have found that a homemade jar of preserves is a welcome and treasured gift year-round. Gourmets might especially appreciate our Pomegranate Jelly, 1-2-3 Alarm Jalapeño Jelly, or Lemon Curd.

Jam and Jelly Tips

◆ Do not double recipes.

◆ Do not reduce the quantity of sugar specified in the recipes.

◆ Be sure to use deep 4-quart or larger glass or microwave-safe bowls.

◆ All cooking times given should be regarded as guidelines. You may need to add or subtract cooking time due to brand or wattage differences in microwave ovens. Remember to use the highest power setting — 100%. After jam or jelly mixture has come to a full rolling boil, power may be reduced to 50 to 70% for a gentler boil, if needed.

◆ Wait until the jam or jelly mixture comes to a full rolling boil, as the recipe directs. Be patient!

◆ Jams and jellies need to be stirred to distribute heat. Frequently, jam or jelly mixtures will boil up when stirred—be careful!

◆ Sugar mixtures get very hot, so remember to use pot holders when removing bowls from the microwave oven.

◆ Whenever you add pectin, do so gradually, stirring very well.

◆ Do not attempt to melt paraffin in your microwave oven— paraffin will not melt under microwave energy. The USDA no longer recommends paraffin sealing.

◆ To test jelly for doneness: Dip a metal spoon into boiling jelly; remove and allow the juice to drip from the side of the spoon. As it nears the jelly stage it will drip from the spoon in two drops, ¼ to ½ inch apart; when the jellying point has been reached, the two drops will run together and drop off in one sheet or flake.

◆ You may use a conventional candy or jelly thermometer to test for doneness instead of the jelly test. Be sure, however, to test with the microwave power off. Do not leave the thermometer in the microwave oven with the power on. At sea level, the jellying point is reached at 220° to 222°F. At higher altitudes it is reached at lower temperatures.

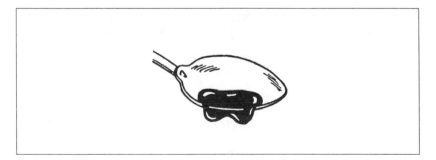

Appearance of jelly that has reached the jellying point.

◆ The U.S. Department of Agriculture recommends storing jams in sterilized jars with two-part lids and processing them in a boiling-water bath. See the following table for processing times.

Recommended Process Times for Jellies and Jams with Added Pectin in a Boiling Water-bath Canner				
Style of Pack	Jar Size	Process time at altitudes of:		
		0-1,000 ft.	1,000-6,000 ft.	Above 6,000 ft.
Hot	Half-pint	5 minutes	10 minutes	15 minutes

Alternatives to Sugar and Pectin in Jams and Jellies

Jams, jellies, preserves, and fruit sauces can be made sugar-free with great results. Sometimes freezer jams don't thicken quite as well when made without sugar. To compensate for this, increase the amount of pectin or use other thickeners, such as tapioca flour or starch, agar-agar (a natural gel made from seaweed), arrowroot powder, or cornstarch. Or simply increase the cooking time, a technique known as *cooking down* or *jamming*.

Jam thickens as it cools. One way to test the consistency of jam while it is cooking is to dip a spoon into the simmering jam to see if it coats the spoon. Add thickener *after* the jam has been partially reduced through cooking. If you use tapioca flour as a thickener, combine it with a little cold water *before* adding it to the jam.

There are no specific rules to follow when substituting honey for sugar in a standard canning recipe. Generally, you'll want to use about half as much honey as sugar, but often less is required, depending on one's individual taste. Choose a mild-flavored honey or use a pure maple syrup. Because it is so concentrated, we recommend using about half as much maple syrup as honey; in this small quantity, it won't change the taste of the fruit.

If fruit is sweet, another option is to prepare the recipe without any sweetener. Follow the cooking down (see Glossary) technique, until desired consistency is reached.

Concentrated fruit juices such as apple, pear, white grape, or a combination of juices may be substituted for sugar. For best results, follow the honey substitution directions.

DECRYSTALLIZING HONEY

To decrystallize honey, place it in the microwave oven (making sure the container is microwave-safe). Insert food probe or microwave-safe food thermometer and microwave on HIGH (100% power) to 120°F. Watch carefully—this goes quickly! Allow 10 to 15 seconds per ¼ cup of honey to decrystallize.

Traditional Berry Freezer Jam

Blackberries, blueberries, boysenberries, gooseberries, huckleberries, loganberries, marionberries, raspberries, or strawberries will all work well in this recipe. Makes about 6 half-pints.

4 cups slightly crushed fresh berries*
4 cups granulated sugar
2 tablespoons lemon juice
3 ounces liquid pectin

Combine berries, sugar, and lemon juice in a deep 3-quart or larger microwave-safe bowl. Microwave for 7 minutes on HIGH (100% power); stir well to combine. Continue cooking on HIGH power for 5 to 8 minutes more, stirring once halfway through cooking time. Mixture should come to a full boil.

Remove from microwave oven and stir in pectin, making sure it is well combined. Let cool 2 to 3 minutes. Fill containers, leaving a 1-inch headspace, seal, and store.

For immediate use: Refrigerate; keeps several weeks.

For longer storage: Cool to room temperature, then freeze.

* Frozen berries may be used, but cooking time will increase by 4 to 6 minutes. If using frozen berries, defrost in microwave on DEFROST (30% power). One quart (4 cups) takes 5 to 6 minutes. Let rest for 5 minutes after defrosting.

Fresh-and-Natural Berry Jam

This natural-style jam has a looser consistency than a conventional jam. It contains no sugar and can be made with any edible cane berries, such as blackberries or raspberries, as well as with strawberries, blueberries, huckleberries, or gooseberries. If berries are tart, increase sweetener to taste. Makes 2 pints.

4 cups berries
¼ to ½ cup honey
⅛ cup pure maple syrup

Wash and stem berries and place them in a large mixing bowl. Crush berries with a potato masher and set aside.

In a 2-cup glass measure combine honey and maple syrup. Microwave on MEDIUM-HIGH (70% power) for 30 to 45 seconds, or until mixture is hot but not boiling. Stir. Pour immediately over crushed berries, stirring well to combine. Ladle into refrigerator or freezer containers as desired.

For immediate use: Seal and refrigerate up to 2 to 3 weeks.

For longer storage: Freeze, leaving ½-inch headspace.

Low-sugar Berry Freezer Jam

Blackberries, blueberries, boysenberries, gooseberries, huckleberries, loganberries, marionberries, raspberries, or strawberries will all work well in this recipe. Makes about 2 half-pints.

2 cups slightly crushed fresh berries*
1 tablespoon powdered pectin
1 cup granulated sugar
1 tablespoon lemon juice

Combine berries and pectin in a large microwave-safe mixing bowl. Microwave on HIGH (100% power) for 5 minutes, stirring once (the mixture should boil). Add the sugar and lemon juice; stir. Microwave on HIGH 7 to 9 minutes more, stirring every few minutes, until mixture comes to a full boil and boils for 1 minute.

For immediate use: Refrigerate up to 2 weeks.

For longer storage: Freeze, leaving a 1-inch headspace.

* Frozen berries may be used, but cooking time will increase by 3 to 4 minutes.

Low-sugar Cherry Freezer Jam

Use any variety of sweet cherries for this delicious jam. Makes about 2 half-pints.

2 cups slightly crushed, pitted fresh sweet cherries*
1 tablespoon powdered pectin
1 cup granulated sugar
1 tablespoon lemon juice

Combine cherries and pectin in a 3-quart microwave-safe bowl or batter bowl. Microwave on HIGH (100% power) for 5 minutes, stirring once halfway through cooking time. Mixture should come to a boil. Add sugar and lemon juice; stir. Microwave on HIGH for 7 to 9 minutes more, stirring every few minutes, until mixture comes to a full boil and boils for 1 minute. Cool slightly and ladle into containers.

For immediate use: Refrigerate up to 2 weeks.

For longer storage: Freeze, leaving a 1-inch headspace.

   * Frozen pitted cherries may be used, but cooking time will increase by 3 to 4 minutes.

PREVENTING BOIL-OVERS

When microwaving jams, jellies, or sauces, use a large, deep bowl or casserole. To prevent a boil-over, turn off the power. Remember that boiling will stop immediately when the microwave power is interrupted.

Berry-Wine Jam

A refreshing and not-so-sweet jam that makes a great gift. Black-berries, loganberries, raspberries, strawberries, blueberries, or marionberries may be used in this recipe. Makes about 4 half-pint jars.

2 cups white wine (French Colombard, Riesling, Chablis,
    or a blush wine)
1⅓ cups crushed berries
1 tablespoon lemon juice
1 1¾-ounce package powdered pectin
3 cups granulated sugar

In a 3- to 4-quart microwave-safe mixing bowl combine all ingredients except sugar. Stir to mix well. Microwave on HIGH (100% power) until mixture boils and pectin is dissolved, about 6 minutes. Stir once halfway through.

Stir in sugar; microwave on HIGH power until mixture returns to a boil, about 6 minutes, stirring once halfway through. Boil on HIGH for 1 minute more. Skim off any foam and ladle into hot, sterile jars. Seal and process in a boiling-water bath (see chart on page 50).

Currant Jelly

Tangy and refreshing, Currant Jelly is a classic that is easy to make in your microwave oven. Makes about 4 half-pints.

Extracting Juice from Currants

8 cups fresh currants, with stems
½ cup water

Wash currants and place them in a deep 3- to 4-quart or larger microwave-safe bowl. Add water; cover with plastic wrap, leaving a side vent. Microwave on HIGH (100% power) for 8 to 10 minutes, or until mixture reaches a boil, stirring halfway through cooking time.

Place colander or sieve over a large bowl. Put jelly bag inside colander and pour slightly cooled currant mixture into bag. Gently press out all juice. Discard stems and seeds. Measure currant juice, adding a small amount of water, if needed, to make 2 cups of juice. The juice may be frozen at this point for later use in jelly making.

Making Jelly

2 cups currant juice
3 cups granulated sugar
3 ounces liquid pectin

In a 3- to 4-quart microwave-safe bowl, combine juice and sugar. Microwave on HIGH (100% power) for 5 minutes; stir and continue microwaving on HIGH for 5 to 7 minutes more, or until mixture comes to a boil. Stir in pectin and microwave on HIGH for 4 to 6 minutes, or until mixture returns to a full boil. Continue microwaving for 1 minute more at a full boil. Skim off any foam. Ladle into hot, sterile jars, seal, and process in a boiling-water bath (see chart on page 50).

Variation

Sweet Cherry Jelly. Substitute 2 pounds fresh sweet cherries, such as Bing, Royal Anne, or Vans, for currants. Wash and stem cherries and proceed as directed.

Plum Jelly

While any kind of plum may be used for this recipe, our favorite is the small Japanese plum. A great gift for gourmets, tangy Japanese Plum Jelly is a rare treat. Makes about 4 half-pints.

Extracting Juice from Plums

2 pounds fresh plums
½ cup water

Wash plums; drain well. Place plums in a deep 3-quart or larger microwave-safe bowl. Crush plums with a potato masher; add water. Microwave on HIGH (100% power) for 10 to 15 minutes, or until mixture comes to a boil, stirring occasionally. Boil 1 minute on HIGH.

   Place colander or sieve over a large bowl. Pour cooled plum mixture into colander. Press out all the juice. Discard pits and pulp. Rinse colander and place jelly bag or muslin cloth inside. Set colander over a large bowl and pour juice through to strain. Do not press pulp through cloth. Measure plum juice, adding a small amount of water, if needed, to make 2 cups of juice. (The juice may be frozen at this point for later use in jelly making.)

Making Jelly

2 cups plum juice
3½ cups sugar
3 ounces liquid pectin

In a deep 3-quart or larger microwave-safe bowl, thoroughly combine juice and sugar. Microwave on HIGH (100% power) for 5 minutes; stir and continue microwaving on HIGH 5 to 7 minutes more, or until mixture comes to a boil. Stir in pectin and microwave on HIGH for 4 to 6 minutes, or until mixture returns to a full boil. Continue microwaving 1 additional minute at a full boil. Skim off any foam. Ladle into hot, sterile jelly jars, seal, and process in a boiling-water bath (see chart on page 50).

Pomegranate Jelly

This rich crimson jelly makes an elegant gift if you can bear to give it away. Makes about 4 half-pint jars.

5 to 6 large pomegranates
½ cup water
1 tablespoon lemon juice
3 cups granulated sugar
3 ounces liquid pectin

Wash pomegranates. Trim crowns and bases, then cut into quarters. Pull back and remove one membrane at a time, exposing clusters of seeds. Gently pull seeds away from white centers. Place all seeds in a bowl. Add ½ cup water. Discard all white membranes, centers, and peel. Place bowl of seeds in microwave oven and cook on HIGH (100% power) for 5 minutes to assist in releasing juice.

Use a food mill or a potato masher to crush seeds and extract juice. If using a potato masher, take a square of waxed paper and poke potato masher handle through the center of the waxed paper. Using waxed paper as a shield, mash seeds with potato masher to release juice. Measure juice, adding a small amount of water, if needed, to make 4 cups. (If there is not enough juice, prepare more, or mix a small amount of water with the pulp left in the food mill and grind again.) Pour juice through a fine strainer into a deep 4-quart or larger glass bowl to remove any seeds or large pieces. Add lemon juice and sugar to pomegranate juice and stir to combine.

Microwave on HIGH for 8 to 10 minutes, or until mixture comes to a full boil. Stir in liquid pectin. Microwave on HIGH until mixture comes to a full boil again; continue to microwave for 1 minute at a full boil. Stir carefully. Skim off any foam with a metal spoon. Pour hot jelly into sterile jars, seal, and process in a boiling-water bath (see chart on page 50).

Juice Jelly

This versatile jelly can be made with apple juice, grape juice, cranberry juice, or cranapple juice cocktail. Makes about 4 half-pint jars.

2 cups juice
3½ cups sugar
3 ounces liquid pectin

Combine juice and sugar in a deep 4-quart or larger microwave-safe bowl. Stir to mix well. Microwave, uncovered, on HIGH (100% power) until mixture comes to a full boil, about 12 to 14 minutes, stirring halfway through cooking time. After mixture has come to a full boil, stir in pectin. Microwave on HIGH, bringing mixture back to a full boil. Time at full boil for 1 minute. Skim off any foam with a metal spoon. Pour jelly into hot, sterile jars, seal, and process in a boiling-water bath (see page 50).

Variations

Mint Jelly. Prepare jelly with apple juice as directed. After skimming, add ½ teaspoon mint extract or 1 drop mint oil and 6 to 8 drops green food coloring (optional). Stir to mix, then pour into hot, sterile jars, and proceed as directed.

Rose Geranium Jelly. Add 4 rose geranium leaves to apple juice and sugar before cooking. Prepare as directed, removing leaves before ladling into hot sterile jars.

Wine Jelly

You may use any burgundy, champagne, port, red, rosé, white, or blush wine you like in this recipe. Wine jellies are good served with beef, pork, lamb, or duck. They can also be spread over cream cheese and served with crackers or bread. Makes about 4 half-pint jars.

1¾ cups wine
3 cups sugar
3 ounces liquid pectin

In a deep microwave-safe mixing bowl, combine wine and sugar. Microwave on HIGH (100% power) for 5 minutes. Stir and continue to microwave until mixture begins to boil (about 4 to 5 minutes more). Time for 1 minute at a full boil. Stir; slowly add pectin, stirring to mix well. Skim, ladle into hot, sterile jars, seal, and process in a boiling-water bath (see chart on page 50).

For something elegant try one of these presentations:

◆ Ladle hot jelly into sterile, stemmed wine glasses. Cover with a small piece of plastic wrap and cool. Use when cooled and set, or refrigerate.

◆ Place small washed bunches of fresh grapes in hot, sterile custard cups. Ladle hot jelly over grapes. Cover with a small piece of plastic wrap and cool. Use when cooled and set, or refrigerate. Do not keep these for more than one month as grapes will not hold.

1-2-3-Alarm Jalapeño Jelly

A colorful hors d'oeuvre served over cream cheese with crackers. This jelly makes a lovely gift and can be as hot or as mild as you wish—just choose the "alarm" you want. Makes 4 half-pint jars.

2 large green bell peppers,* washed and seeded
1 jalapeño pepper,** washed and seeded
4 cups granulated sugar
¾ cup white or white-wine vinegar
3 ounces liquid pectin
3 to 4 drops green food coloring (optional)

Puree or grind all peppers together. You should have 1½ cups. Mix ground peppers and their juices with sugar and vinegar in a large, deep microwave-safe bowl. Cover with waxed paper and microwave on HIGH (100% power) for 10 to 12 minutes, stirring halfway through. Remove waxed paper and microwave for 1 to 2 more minutes, bringing to a boil. Add pectin; stir well. Microwave 2 minutes more. Stir in food coloring if desired. Skim, pour into hot, sterile jars, seal, and process in a boiling-water bath (see chart on page 50) .

* You may substitute red, yellow, or orange peppers for color and taste variations (all delicious).

** Adjust hotness of jelly as follows:

    1-Alarm (mild): 1 jalapeño pepper

    2-Alarm (medium): 2 jalapeño peppers

    3-Alarm (hot): 3 jalapeño peppers

All-American Apple Butter

Making apple butter was a very time-consuming task before this micro-wave method simplified the process. Apricots, crab apples, figs, peaches, pears, or plums can be substituted for apples. Makes 4 half-pint jars.

8 cups peeled, cored, and chopped apples (1-inch chunks)
1 cup apple cider or juice
2 cups granulated sugar*
1 teaspoon ground cinnamon**
½ teaspoon ground cloves**

Combine apples and cider in a 4-quart or larger microwave-safe bowl. Cover and microwave on HIGH (100% power) for 10 to 12 minutes, stirring with a wooden spoon every 3 minutes. Process cooked apples to a pulplike consistency in a blender or food processor. Return apple pulp to mixing bowl and stir in sugar and spices.

Microwave, uncovered, on HIGH for 15 to 20 minutes, stirring every 5 minutes. Check consistency. Cooking times for butters are not as precise as those for jams and jellies; allow additional cooking time if necessary. Ladle hot apple butter into hot, sterile jars, leaving a ¼-inch headspace; seal.

For immediate use: Let cool; refrigerate for 1 month or more.

For longer storage: Process sealed jars conventionally in a boiling-water bath for 10 minutes.

* You may adjust the recipe to your taste, using less sugar or honey if you wish.

** If you prefer to use whole spices instead of ground, tie whole cinnamon and cloves in a muslin bag or cloth. Combine with apples and cider for first cooking. Be sure to remove the bag after the first cooking step. Proceed as directed. Note that the taste of spices tends to be strongest just after cooking; it will mellow after a day or two.

Lemon Curd

This traditional English spread has a saucelike consistency. Serve this tart-sweet, creamy treat as you would any jam. It is especially good on hot scones or gingerbread or as a cake filling. Makes 1½ cups.

6 tablespoons butter or margarine
¾ cup granulated sugar
2 teaspoons grated lemon rind
¼ cup lemon juice
3 eggs, beaten

Place butter in a large glass measure or bowl. Microwave on HIGH (100% power) for 10 seconds, or until butter is soft but not melted. Stir or whisk in sugar, lemon rind, and juice. Add eggs and blend well. Cover with waxed paper and microwave on HIGH for 3 minutes, stirring every minute.

Pour mixture into a sterilized container, cover, and let cool. Curd will become thicker upon standing.

For immediate use: Refrigerate up to 1 week.

For longer storage: Freeze, leaving 1-inch headspace; use within 3 months.

Variations

Lemon Curd with Honey. Substitute ½ cup of honey for the ¾ cup sugar. Proceed as directed.

Lime or Orange Curd. Substitute lime or orange juice and rind for lemon. Proceed as directed.

JUICY LEMONS, LIMES, OR ORANGES

To release more juice from these citrus fruits, place them, one at a time, in microwave oven and microwave on HIGH (100% power) for 30 seconds. Cut and squeeze as usual.

Lemon-Curd Pie or Tarts

This easy but superbly delicious recipe uses Lemon Curd as its primary ingredient. Makes one 9-inch pie or 6 tarts.

1½ cups Lemon Curd (see page 63), cooled
1½ cups sweetened whipped cream
1 9-inch baked pie shell or 6 tart shells*
thin lemon slices for garnish
¼ cup toasted coconut (optional)

In a large mixing bowl, gently fold Lemon Curd and whipped cream. Spoon into pie shell or tart shells. Garnish with lemon slices. Chill for 1 hour. Sprinkle with toasted coconut, if desired; serve.

   * You may use a cookie-crumb, graham-cracker, or traditional flour crust.

TOASTING COCONUT

It's easy to toast coconut in the microwave oven. Spread ½ cup flaked coconut on a pie plate or a paper plate. Microwave on HIGH (100% power), uncovered, for 3 to 4 minutes, stirring after 2 minutes, and every 30 seconds thereafter, or until coconut turns a light golden brown.

Apricot-Nut Conserve

This colorful and unusual conserve can be made with peaches or nectarines if you prefer. An excellent gift. Makes 6 half-pint jars.

3 cups apricots, pitted and quartered

1 cup crushed pineapple, drained

3½ cups granulated sugar

¼ cup lemon juice or fruit liqueur (lemon, apricot, peach, or orange)

3 ounces liquid pectin

½ cup chopped nuts (walnuts or pecans are excellent)

Combine fruits with sugar and lemon juice, if used, in a deep 4- to 5-quart microwave-safe bowl. (If using liqueur, do not add it at this time.) Microwave on HIGH (100% power) for 15 minutes, stirring every 5 minutes. Microwave 1 to 2 minutes more to bring to a boil. Stir in liqueur, if using. Stir in pectin and skim off any foam. Stir in nuts. Ladle into hot, sterile jars, seal, and process in a boiling-water bath (see chart on page 50).

PEELING PEACHES, NECTARINES, OR APRICOTS

Bring 2 cups of water to a boil in a 4-cup glass measure on HIGH (100% power) (about 4 to 5 minutes). Remove boiling water from microwave. Spear whole fruit with a fork and hold it under the hot water for 30 seconds. Quickly cool fruit under cold tap water or in a bowl of ice water. Peel.

For larger quantities, increase size of container, amount of water, and cooking time. Place several whole fruits in water that has just boiled. Remove after 1 minute, place in ice water, and peel. Reheat water as necessary by microwaving on HIGH until water boils. (*Note:* If fruit is underripe, it may need additional time in the boiling water.)

Lemony Fig Conserve

Our taste-testers declared this conserve a winner! It has a wonderful tart-sweet flavor that even non–fig lovers will like. Makes about 2 half-pints.

1 cup (8 ounces) whole dried figs
Zest of 1 lemon
½ cup lemon juice
1 tablespoon water
¾ cup granulated sugar
¼ cup slivered almonds, chopped walnuts, or chopped pecans

Trim stems from figs. Dice figs. Cut lemon zest into thin strips or slivers. Combine all ingredients except nuts in a 3-quart microwave-safe mixing bowl.

Microwave on HIGH (100% power) for 6 minutes, stirring halfway through. Remove from microwave oven and stir in nuts. Ladle into hot sterile jars; seal.

For immediate use: Cool and refrigerate up to 4 to 6 weeks.

For longer storage: Process in a boiling-water bath (see chart on page 50).

 BLANCHING ALMONDS AND/OR HAZELNUTS (FILBERTS)
Measure 1 cup hot tap water in a 4-cup glass measure. Microwave on HIGH (100% power) for 1½ minutes, or until water comes to a boil. Add 1 cup shelled, unblanched nuts. Microwave mixture for 1 minute on HIGH power. Drain; place nuts on paper towels to cool slightly. Rub with hands or towels; skins will slip off.

Rhubarb Conserve

A true delight! Make extra for gifts. Yields about 2 half-pints.

2 cups sliced rhubarb
1¼ cups granulated sugar
½ cup golden raisins
2 tablespoons orange juice
1 tablespoon lemon juice
1½ teaspoons orange zest, thinly sliced
1½ teaspoons lemon zest, thinly sliced
¼ cup chopped walnuts, hazelnuts, or pecans

Combine all ingredients except nuts in a 3- to 4-quart microwave-safe bowl. Stir to combine. Microwave on HIGH (100% power) for 6 minutes, or until mixture comes to a boil; stirring once halfway through.

Reduce power to MEDIUM (50%) and microwave for 7 minutes, or until mixture has thickened slightly. Stir in nuts. Ladle into hot sterile jars, seal, and process in a boiling-water bath (see chart on page 50).

Orange Marmalade

Freshly squeezed orange juice is the secret to this lovely marmalade. Makes about 4 half-pints.

½ orange
2 cups fresh orange juice
3½ cups granulated sugar
3 ounces liquid pectin

Cut entire peel off orange half. Set aside orange sections for another use. Cut peel into thin strips. Cut each strip into small pieces.

Place all ingredients except pectin in a 3- to 4-quart microwave-safe bowl. Stir to combine. Microwave, uncovered, on HIGH (100% power) for 10 to 12 minutes, or until mixture comes to a boil, stirring halfway through cooking time. After mixture has come to a full boil, stir in pectin. Microwave on HIGH, bringing back to a full boil. Time at full boil for 1 minute. Skim off any foam, pour into hot, sterile jars, and seal. Process in a boiling-water bath (see chart on page 50).

Easy Strawberry-Rhubarb Preserves

An easy and unusual recipe that calls for gelatin as a thickener. A colorful treat. Makes about 5 half-pints.

5 cups thinly sliced rhubarb
3 cups sugar
1 6-ounce package strawberry gelatin

Combine sliced rhubarb and sugar in a 3- to 4-quart microwave-safe bowl. Stir and let stand, covered, overnight.

Stir again and cover with plastic wrap, leaving a side vent. Microwave on HIGH (100% power) for 8 to 10 minutes, or until mixture reaches a full boil, stirring twice during cooking time. Remove plastic wrap and stir in gelatin. Ladle into hot sterile jars. Seal and let stand overnight. These preserves will thicken as they cool. Refrigerate.

Variation

Strawberry-Lemon or Strawberry-Orange Preserves. Substitute lemon- or orange-flavored gelatin for the strawberry gelatin. Proceed as directed.

Classic Strawberry-Rhubarb Preserves

This classic combination of fruits has a slightly lower sugar content than most preserves, which makes the fruit flavor more dominant. Makes about 5 half-pints.

4 cups (1 pound) rhubarb, sliced ¼ inch thick
2 cups (1 pint) thickly sliced strawberries
4 cups granulated sugar

Combine all ingredients in a 4-quart or larger microwave-safe bowl. Stir gently to mix well and cover with plastic wrap, leaving vent. Microwave on HIGH (100% power) for 10 minutes, stirring halfway through cooking time. Mixture should come to a boil. Stir and remove cover. Microwave uncovered on HIGH for 10 to 15 minutes more, stirring every 5 minutes. Skim off foam. Ladle preserves into hot, sterile jars and seal. Process in a boiling-water bath (see chart on page 50).

Kiwi-Pineapple Preserves

These unusual preserves have a lovely color and taste. Makes 4 half-pint jars.

¼ cup lime juice
½ cup unsweetened crushed pineapple, drained
2½ cups granulated sugar
4 kiwis, washed, peeled, and sliced ⅛ inch thick
3 ounces liquid pectin

In a 3- to 4-quart microwave-safe mixing bowl, place lime juice, pineapple, and sugar; stir to combine. Microwave on HIGH (100% power) for 6 minutes, stirring once halfway through cooking time. Add kiwi, stirring in gently. Microwave on HIGH for 2 minutes. Stir and continue microwaving for 2 to 3 minutes more, or until mixture comes to a full boil. Immediately stir in pectin. Skim off any foam. Ladle mixture into hot, sterile jars; seal. Process in a boiling-water bath (see chart on page 50).

Variation

Kiwi-Strawberry Preserves. Substitute ¼ cup lemon juice for the lime juice and ½ cup sliced or chopped strawberries (fresh or frozen*) for the pineapple. Increase the quantity of sugar to 3 cups. Proceed as directed.

* If using whole frozen strawberries, microwave on HIGH for 1 minute, then slice or chop.

Old-fashioned Tomato Preserves

These have the true old-fashioned flavor of Grandmother's tomato preserves but can be made in a fraction of the time! Makes about 2 half-pints.

½ lemon
½ orange
2 cups granulated sugar
4 cups peeled and chopped red, yellow, or green
   tomatoes (about 6 medium-large tomatoes)
2 cinnamon sticks
4 whole cloves

Finely shred zest from orange and lemon halves. Place in a deep 3- to 4-quart microwave-safe bowl. Add sugar and juices (with pulp) with orange and lemon halves. Microwave on HIGH (100% power) for 5 to 6 minutes, stirring every 2 minutes. Stir in remaining ingredients; microwave on HIGH for 30 to 35 minutes, stirring every 5 minutes. Ladle into hot sterile jars, seal, and process in a boiling-water bath (see chart on page 50).

 To renew crystallized preserves, remove lid from glass jar and microwave on HIGH (100% power) for 1 minute.

Berry Syrup

Fresh-fruit syrups are great on pancakes or waffles! Choose blueberries, blackberries, boysenberries, elderberries, huckleberries, marionberries, loganberries, raspberries, or strawberries to make this super syrup. Makes about 1 pint.

1 quart (about 1 pound) whole berries, washed and stemmed
1½ to 2 cups granulated sugar (depending upon
   sweetness of berries)
1 teaspoon lemon juice

Place berries in blender or food processor; puree. Transfer berries to a 3- to 4-quart microwave-safe bowl. Add remaining ingredients and stir to combine. Microwave on HIGH (100% power) for 7 to 8 minutes, or until mixture comes to a full boil.

Reduce power to MEDIUM (50%) for 5 minutes, stirring once halfway through cooking time. Cool. Serve as is, or for a clear syrup, strain through a jelly bag (see page 56). Place in a sterile jar, seal, and refrigerate.

Variation

Sweet Cherry Syrup. Substitute an equal amount of sweet cherries (any variety) for the berries. Wash, stem, and pit cherries and proceed as directed.

FIVE

Pickles, Relishes, and Condiments

Microwave preserving techniques shine when it comes to preparing pickles, relishes, and condiments. Pickle brines are a cinch to make, and relishes and condiments don't require constant "pot-watching" to avoid scorching. Old-fashioned slow-cooking preparations, such as Heather's Mild Chili Sauce and Tomato Butter, can be made in less than half the conventional cooking time.

When longer shelf-storage is desired, we and the USDA Extension Service recommend a boiling-water bath for pickles, relishes, and condiments. Note that this is a conventional, not a microwave, process.

Pickling Tips

Salt: When a pickle recipe calls for salt, be sure to use pure, granulated pickling salt or uniodized table salt. Pickling salt is preferable. Table salt, even if uniodized, contains an anticaking ingredient that may make the brine cloudy. Iodized salt can also make pickles darken.

Vinegar: Select a high-grade vinegar with an acidity level of 4 to 6 percent (40- to 60-grain vinegar). Cider vinegar is used for most pickles. Distilled white vinegar may be substituted for cider vinegar, especially when a lighter-colored pickled product is desired. Vinegar provides that special tangy tartness to pickles and relishes as well as acting as a preservative. Do not dilute vinegar; follow recipes exactly.

Sugar: Sugar balances the tartness of the vinegar. It will also give you a milder-flavored pickle. If a milder pickle is desired, add sugar to the pickling solution instead of diluting the vinegar.

Granulated white sugar is used for most pickles and is preferred for light-colored pickles. Packed brown sugar may be used for darker varieties of pickles for its special flavor.

Water: If your water is exceptionally hard, you may wish to use distilled water for better pickle making. The minerals in hard water will settle to the bottom of the jar after processing.

English Mint Sauce

A classic meat condiment from England. Makes about ⅔ cup.

3 tablespoons water
2 tablespoons sugar
⅓ cup finely chopped fresh mint leaves *or* ¼ cup dried mint leaves
⅓ cup vinegar (white-wine or champagne vinegar preferred)
1 to 2 drops green food coloring (optional)

In a 2-cup glass measure combine water and sugar. Microwave on HIGH (100% power) for 45 seconds. Stir to make sure sugar is well dissolved. Allow to cool. Add remaining ingredients. Stir well and allow to rest ½ hour before serving.

For longer storage: Place sauce in a tightly-capped glass bottle and store in refrigerator indefinitely.

Home-style
Bread-and-Butter Pickles

Everyone loves these mild and fresh-tasting favorites. Makes 4 pints.

2½ pounds pickling cucumbers, washed, trimmed, and sliced
1 small onion, peeled and sliced into rings
Ice water
1½ cups cider vinegar
1½ cups water
1½ cups granulated sugar
1½ teaspoons celery seed
1½ teaspoons mustard seed
¾ teaspoon pickling salt
¾ teaspoon dill seed

Place sliced cucumbers and onion rings in a 4-quart or larger microwave-safe bowl. Cover with ice water. Soak until crisp, at least 1 hour. Microwave on HIGH (100% power), covered for 7 to 8 minutes, or until 110°F.* Stir twice during cooking time. Drain and pack in clean jars.

Combine remaining ingredients in a 3-quart or larger microwave-safe mixing bowl. Microwave on HIGH for 10 minutes, or until mixture comes to a full boil, stirring every 3 minutes. Pour hot mixture over cucumber-and-onion mixture in jars. Seal.

For immediate use: Let age 24 to 48 hours in refrigerator before using. Keeps 1 month or more in refrigerator.

For longer storage: Process pint jars conventionally in a boiling-water bath for 10 minutes.

* If you have a microwave-safe thermometer, place it in the mixture and check temperature. If you have a microwave temperature probe, place probe in center of mixture and set temperature for 110°F. Timing is then automatic. If you do not have either of these, check temperature periodically with a conven-

tional thermometer by stopping the microwave oven and insert-
ing thermometer in center of mixture. Do not leave thermometer
in mixture while cooking unless it is safe for microwave use.

Easy Candied Dill Pickles

A shortcut recipe for an old-fashioned American favorite. Makes 2 pints.

1 quart dill pickles*
3 cups granulated sugar
⅔ cup white vinegar
2 tablespoons mixed pickling spices

Drain dill pickles, discarding liquid with spices. Cut whole pickles into strips lengthwise. Pack pickles in pint jars. Set aside
until syrup is made.

Combine sugar, vinegar, and pickling spices in a large glass
mixing bowl. Microwave on HIGH (100% power) for 2 minutes; stir and microwave 1 to 2 minutes more, or until mixture
comes to a full boil. Stir. Let cool slightly.

Strain off pickling spices and pour warm syrup over pickle
strips. Seal and store in refrigerator 1 week before using. Keeps
4 to 6 weeks in refrigerator.

* Use regular dill, not kosher/deli dill pickles, for best
results.

Sweet Mixed Pickles

Make these classic pickles and keep your kitchen cool with this microwave method. Makes 3 pints.

1 pound pickling cucumbers, sliced ½-inch thick (2 cups, total)
2 cups cauliflower florets
1 large sweet red pepper, seeded and cut into 1-inch chunks
1 cup peeled tiny onions*
¼ cup pickling salt
3 cups white or cider vinegar
1 cup granulated sugar
¾ cup packed light brown or raw sugar
¼ teaspoon turmeric
1 tablespoon mixed pickling spices
1 whole cinnamon stick, broken in half
6 whole cloves
1 teaspoon mustard seed

Combine vegetables and sprinkle with pickling salt. Cover with cold water. Place lid or plastic wrap over container and refrigerate overnight.

Drain off salted water; rinse with fresh water and drain well. Combine vinegar, sugar, and turmeric in a large microwave-safe mixing bowl. Stir to dissolve sugar. Place remaining spices in a muslin bag and add to vinegar mixture. Microwave on HIGH (100% power) for 15 to 18 minutes or until mixture comes to a boil. Stir twice during cooking time.

After mixture has reached a boil, lower power setting to MEDIUM-HIGH (70%) and microwave for 10 minutes, stirring twice.

Add drained vegetables (and frozen tiny onions, if used) to hot vinegar mixture. Microwave on HIGH just until mixture comes to a boil, about 10 to 12 minutes. Remove and discard spice bag. Ladle hot pickle mixture into hot, sterile jars, leaving a ½-inch headspace. Seal jars.

For immediate use: Let cool and refrigerate. Keeps 1 month or more.

For longer storage: Process sealed jars conventionally in a boiling-water bath for 5 minutes. Check seals; cool and store.

* If using frozen tiny onions, do not let stand overnight in salted water. Add as directed.

SOFTENING BROWN SUGAR

If your box of brown sugar is hard, you can soften and freshen the brown sugar by placing the entire box in the microwave oven and heating it on HIGH (100% power) for about 20 seconds. (Time will vary slightly depending upon the amount of sugar in the box.)

To keep brown sugar soft, add one slice of apple peel to box or container of brown sugar. The apple peel will not spoil but will dry in the brown sugar while keeping it moist.

Watermelon Pickles

We developed this recipe at the request — no, insistence — of Cheryl's mother. (She loves them!) They became a new favorite with our families. (Grandmother knows best.) We hope you will like them as much as we do. Makes 3 half-pint jars.

5 cups watermelon rind
5 cups water
¼ cup pickling salt
2 cups granulated sugar
1 cup white vinegar
Muslin spice bag containing:
   3 cinnamon sticks, broken in half
   2 teaspoons whole cloves
   ½ teaspoon mustard seed

Remove all green or outer rind and pink inner portions from watermelon. The firm white or greenish-white layer of the watermelon is what is used. Cut into 1-inch cubes. Place in a large mixing bowl and add water and salt. Stir to combine, being careful not to mash cubes. Cover; let stand overnight.

Drain off salted water from cubed watermelon rind. Add warm water until watermelon rind is just covered. Microwave, covered, on HIGH (100% power) until mixture just comes to a boil. (Time will vary depending upon the starting temperature of the warm water.) Reduce power to MEDIUM-HIGH (70%) and microwave for 2 to 3 minutes. Drain off water and set watermelon rind aside.

In a 2-quart microwave-safe mixing bowl, combine sugar and vinegar. Add spice bag and microwave on HIGH for 4 to 5 minutes, or until mixture comes to a full boil. Set aside for 15 minutes.

Add drained watermelon rind to liquid mixture. Microwave on HIGH until mixture comes to a boil, about 4 to 5 minutes. Stir gently; remove and discard spice bag. Microwave on MEDIUM-HIGH up to 5 to 6 minutes more, or until fruit is clear and slightly transparent. Pack hot mixture immediately into hot, sterile jars. Seal.

For immediate use: Cool and refrigerate. Keeps several months.

For longer storage: Process in a boiling-water bath for 5 minutes.

No-fail Dill Pickles

This easy recipe hasn't failed yet! Summer-fresh dill pickles made coolly in your kitchen with a microwave assist. Makes two 1-quart jars.

2 quarts fresh cucumbers
4 to 8 heads fresh dill, to taste
3 garlic cloves, peeled and minced
1 cup vinegar
3 cups water
1/4 cup pickling salt

Wash and trim cucumbers and prick them once with a fork. Pack cucumbers in sterilized quart jars, leaving a 1/2-inch headspace. Sprinkle chopped dill heads and minced garlic throughout as you are packing jars. Set jars aside.

Combine vinegar, water, and pickling salt in a 2-quart microwave-safe batter bowl. Stir to combine. Microwave on HIGH (100% power) for 8 to 9 minutes, or until mixture comes to a boil. Remove, stir, and pour hot brine over cucumbers. Seal jars; let cool.

For immediate use: Place cooled jars in refrigerator and let age 2 weeks before using. Store 6 to 8 weeks in refrigerator.

For longer storage: Process quart jars in a boiling-water bath for 15 minutes.

Helene's Special Mustard Relish

This great relish comes from mustard expert Helene Sawyer, the author of Gourmet Mustards: How to Make and Cook with Them. *It's perfect on hot dogs or in tartar sauce and salad dressings. Finely chop vegetables so they will blend and spread easily — fast work if you have a food processor! Makes 3 pints.*

2 cups finely chopped cabbage (about ½ small head)
2 cups finely chopped cucumber (about 2 medium)
½ cup finely chopped onion
1 cup finely chopped green bell pepper
1 teaspoon turmeric
2 tablespoons uniodized salt
1 quart warm water
2 tablespoons pickling spices
¾ cup packed brown sugar
2 cups cider vinegar
2 tablespoons dry mustard
1½ teaspoons yellow mustard seed
¼ teaspoon ground ginger
½ teaspoon celery seed

Combine cabbage, cucumber, onion, and pepper in a large mixing bowl; sprinkle with turmeric. Dissolve salt in warm water and pour over vegetables; let stand, covered, 3 to 4 hours. Drain off salted water.

Place pickling spices in a small muslin bag. Combine bag, sugar, and vinegar in a 2-quart microwave-safe batter or mixing bowl. Microwave about 5 minutes on HIGH (100% power) until mixture comes to a boil; stir after 3 minutes. Add dry mustard, mustard seed, ginger, and celery seed to vegetables; pour hot spice mixture over vegetables and stir lightly. Cover and let stand overnight in a cool place.

Microwave mixture on HIGH until it comes to a boil. Remove and discard pickling spice bag. Pack hot relish in hot, sterile jars, leaving a ½-inch headspace.

For immediate use: Let cool and refrigerate up to 8 to 10 weeks.
For longer storage: Process sealed jars conventionally in a boiling-water bath for 10 minutes. Check seals, cool, and store.

Calico Sweet-Pickle Relish

This sweet-pickle relish cooks quickly and easily in your microwave oven. Chop vegetables in a food processor to save even more time. Makes 3 pints.

3½ cups finely chopped pickling cucumber (about 6 medium)
2 medium onions, peeled and finely chopped
1 large green bell pepper, seeded and finely chopped
2 medium red bell peppers, seeded and finely chopped
¼ cup pickling or uniodized salt
½ cup cold water
1½ cups granulated sugar
1 cup white or cider vinegar
1 teaspoon mustard seed
1 teaspoon celery seed
¼ teaspoon turmeric

Combine vegetables in a large container and sprinkle with pickling salt. Add ½ cup water; stir to mix well. Place lid or plastic wrap over container and refrigerate overnight.

Drain off salted water. Rinse in fresh water and drain well. In a large microwave-safe mixing bowl, combine sugar, vinegar, and spices, stirring to mix well.

Microwave on HIGH (100% power) for 5 to 6 minutes, or until mixture comes to a boil, stirring twice. Add the drained, chopped vegetables to the vinegar mixture, stirring well to combine. Microwave on HIGH for 6 to 7 minutes, or until mixture comes to a boil, stirring twice. Ladle hot mixture into hot, sterile jars, leaving a ½-inch headspace.

For immediate use: Let cool and refrigerate up to 6 to 8 weeks.
For longer storage: Process pint jars in a boiling-water bath for 10 minutes.

Fresh Tomato Relish

This light relish is great with summer barbecues or as a substitute (with or without variation) for fresh salsa. If you like it spicy, add the larger amounts of mustard and onion. Makes about 1½ pints.

1 to 1½ teaspoons dry mustard
1 teaspoon celery seed
1 teaspoon mustard seed
¾ teaspoon pickling or uniodized salt
¼ teaspoon white pepper
1 tablespoon sugar
2 tablespoons white or white-wine vinegar
3 cups finely chopped tomato
¾ cup finely chopped green bell pepper
⅔ cup finely chopped celery
¼ to ½ cup finely chopped onion

Place all spices, sugar, and vinegar in a 3- to 4-quart microwave-safe bowl. Stir to combine. Microwave on HIGH (100% power) for 1 minute. Add all chopped vegetables, stirring to combine. Microwave on HIGH for 3 minutes. Stir well and refrigerate for at least 1 hour before serving. Store in refrigerator.

Variation

Fresh Salsa. After cooking, add 2 to 3 tablespoons chopped fresh cilantro and Tabasco sauce, to taste. Jalapeño pepper–flavored vinegar may also be substituted for the white vinegar if desired. Proceed as directed.

Zucchini Relish

This tangy relish can be used in place of standard pickle relish. Expect raves! Makes 4 pints.

Vegetables

¼ cup pickling salt
Ice water
3½ to 4 cups finely chopped zucchini (about 3 medium;
   8 to 9 inches long)
2 onions, peeled and finely chopped (about 2½ cups)
1 green bell pepper, seeded, trimmed, and finely chopped
1 red bell pepper, seeded, trimmed, and finely chopped

Pickling Syrup

1½ cups granulated sugar   1 teaspoon celery seed
1¼ cups white or cider vinegar   1 teaspoon turmeric
⅓ cup water   ½ teaspoon mustard seed

In a 6-quart or larger container, dissolve salt in enough ice water to cover vegetables. Add chopped vegetables, stir, and allow to stand for 1 hour.

Drain off salted water; rinse vegetables with cold water. Drain well. Set aside to complete draining as pickling syrup is prepared.

In a 4-quart or larger microwave-safe mixing bowl combine all ingredients for pickling syrup. Stir; cover with plastic wrap. Microwave on HIGH (100% power) for 6 to 7 minutes, or until mixture comes to a boil. Stir, then reduce power to MEDIUM-HIGH (70%) and microwave, uncovered, for 3 minutes.

Carefully add well-drained vegetables to pickling syrup, stirring to combine well. Microwave on HIGH for 10 minutes, or until mixture comes to a boil, stirring twice. Stir and ladle into prepared sterile jars.

For immediate use: Cool and refrigerate jars up to 2 months.

For longer storage: Leave a ½-inch headspace in jars. Process sealed jars in a conventional boiling-water bath for 10 minutes.

Confetti Corn Relish

This delicious old-fashioned relish can be made year-round with canned corn. If using fresh or frozen corn, cook corn before preparing relish. Good as a side dish with meat or poultry; great for picnics. Makes 3 half-pint jars.

⅓ cup granulated sugar

1 tablespoon cornstarch

1 teaspoon mustard seed

1 teaspoon celery seed

¼ teaspoon turmeric

½ cup finely chopped onion

⅓ cup finely chopped green bell pepper

⅓ cup finely chopped red bell pepper

2 tablespoons corn liquid (reserved from canned corn) or water

⅓ cup white or cider vinegar

⅓ cup pickle or zucchini relish

2 cups cooked corn (1 16- to 17-ounce can; drain and
   reserve 2 tablespoons liquid)

In a 2- or 3-quart glass bowl combine all ingredients except corn, mixing well. Cover with plastic wrap and microwave on HIGH (100% power) for 3 minutes. Stir in corn. Microwave on HIGH for 4 minutes more, or until mixture boils and thickens slightly. Stir and ladle into prepared sterile jars. Seal.

For immediate use: Cool, and refrigerate up to 4 weeks.

For longer storage: Process sealed jars in a conventional boiling-water bath for 15 minutes.

Pickled Vegetables

Tender-crisp microwave vegetables work superbly in this dill-flavored recipe. A change of pace for the appetizer or salad buffet. Suggested vegetables: small asparagus spears, green or wax beans, baby or French carrots, or cauliflower (separate into florets). Makes about 2 quarts.

2 pounds fresh vegetables, washed and trimmed

Pickling Brine:

2 cups hot water
2 cups white or white-wine vinegar
⅔ cup granulated sugar
2 tablespoons coarse (Kosher-style) salt
6 whole peppercorns
4 fresh garlic cloves, peeled
2 teaspoons mustard seed
3 teaspoons fresh dill or 2 teaspoons dried dill
¼ teaspoon celery seed

Place trimmed vegetable of choice in casserole or bowl; cover with lid or plastic wrap. Microwave on HIGH (100% power) as follows:

Asparagus: spears, cut into 2- or 3-inch pieces	6 to 8 minutes
Beans: green and/or wax: whole or cut into 3- or 4-inch pieces	10 to 12 minutes
Carrots: French or baby: whole or cut into 1-inch chunks or thin sticks	12 to 14 minutes
Cauliflower: break or cut into florets	7 to 9 minutes

Place cooked vegetable(s) in two sterile 1-quart jars. Set aside.

In a 2-quart microwave-safe batter bowl or mixing bowl combine water, vinegar, sugar, and salt. Stir to combine. Microwave, covered, on HIGH until mixture comes to a boil, about 5 to 6 minutes. Stir.

Divide spices evenly between quart jars. Pour hot vinegar mixture over vegetables. Seal and refrigerate for at least 8 hours before serving. Serve chilled.

For immediate use: Keeps in refrigerator up to 2 weeks.

For longer storage: Process sealed jars in a conventional boiling-water bath for 10 minutes. (Do not refrigerate first if processing; jars should not be cold.)

Quick Pickled Beets

These beets have a spicy-sweet pickled flavor reminiscent of their Scandinavian home-style origins but updated for today's microwave cook. Makes about 1 pint.

1 16-ounce can sliced beets; drain and reserve liquid
⅓ cup sugar
⅓ cup vinegar
¼ teaspoon salt (optional)
4 whole cloves
4 whole allspice berries
1½-inch piece cinnamon stick
½ teaspoon dried minced onion

In a 2-quart glass batter bowl or mixing bowl, combine all ingredients except sliced beets (but including reserved beet liquid). Microwave on HIGH (100% power) for 4 to 5 minutes, or until mixture comes to a full boil, stirring once halfway through cooking time. Remove from microwave oven and add drained sliced beets to liquid mixture; stir gently. Refrigerate in a covered container for 12 to 24 hours before removing whole spices and serving. Serve chilled. Keeps 3 to 4 weeks in the refrigerator.

Heather's Mild Chili Sauce

Heather Kibbey, editor of Oregon Restaurateur *magazine, shared this great family recipe with us. It makes a chunky but juicy chili sauce that is mild, in the English tradition. Thanks to microwave techniques, this recipe produces an even fresher taste than the original. Makes 4 pints.*

4 pounds ripe tomatoes, peeled and coarsely chopped
1 large onion, chopped into ¼-inch pieces
1 cup finely chopped celery
½ green bell pepper, finely chopped
½ red bell pepper, finely chopped
1 medium, firm apple, peeled, seeded, and finely chopped
2 teaspoons pickling salt or uniodized salt
1 rounded tablespoon pickling spices, tied in a muslin bag
⅔ cup granulated sugar
⅔ cup white vinegar

In a 4-quart or larger microwave-safe mixing bowl, combine all ingredients. Microwave on HIGH (100% power) for 35 minutes, stirring every 5 to 10 minutes. Remove and discard spice bag. Ladle mixture into hot, sterile jars and seal.

For immediate use: Let cool and refrigerate. Best after 24 hours. Sauce will keep 4 to 6 weeks in the refrigerator.

For longer storage: Process sealed jars in a conventional water bath for 15 minutes.

PEELING TOMATOES

Bring 2 cups of water to a boil in a 4-cup glass measure on HIGH (100% power) (about 4 to 5 minutes). Remove boiling water from microwave. Spear tomato with a fork and hold it under the hot water for 12 to 15 seconds. Quickly cool tomato under cold tap water or in a bowl of ice water. Peel.

For larger quantities, increase size of container, amount of water, and microwave time. Place several whole tomatoes in water that has just boiled. Remove tomatoes after 20 to 25 seconds, place in ice water, and peel. Reheat water as necessary by microwaving on HIGH until water boils.

Fruity Barbecue Sauce

Fresh summer fruits add a special taste to this succulent sauce. Great on ribs! Can be made with apricots, papayas, peaches, pears, or nectarines. Makes about 3 half-pints.

¼ cup chopped onion
3 cups peeled and sliced fruit*
½ cup sherry
⅔ cup packed dark brown sugar
⅔ cup chili sauce or catsup
¼ cup cider, fruit, or white-wine vinegar
2 teaspoons dry mustard
1 teaspoon Worcestershire sauce
1 tablespoon molasses
½ teaspoon Tabasco sauce
½ teaspoon salt

Place onion in food processor or blender; process until finely chopped. Add fruit and process until pureed.

Combine all ingredients in a 3- to 4-quart (or larger) microwave-safe bowl. Stir. Cover bowl with plastic wrap, leaving vent. Microwave on HIGH (100% power) for 9 to 10 minutes, or until mixture reaches a boil. Stir, reduce power to MEDIUM (50%), and microwave for 15 minutes, uncovered, stirring every 5 minutes. Ladle into sterile containers.

For immediate use: Pour into sterile jars or containers. Keeps several weeks refrigerated.

For longer storage: Let sauce cool slightly before ladling into freezer containers. Seal. Keeps 6 to 8 months frozen.

* If fresh fruit is out of season, frozen or canned fruit may be substituted. Fruit that is unsweetened or packed in natural juice is preferable.

Variation

Rhubarb Barbecue Sauce. Substitute 3 cups chopped rhubarb for other fruit. Increase brown sugar to 1 cup packed. Place rhubarb in a 3- to 4-quart microwave-safe bowl and microwave on HIGH for 5 to 6 minutes, or until tender. Puree rhubarb with finely chopped onion and proceed as directed.

Spicy American Barbecue Sauce

A versatile barbecue sauce that's a perfect complement to meats and poultry. Quick, easy-to-make, and economical, too! Makes 1 pint.

½ cup finely chopped onion
1 peeled, minced garlic clove (optional)
1 8-ounce can tomato sauce
½ cup chili sauce
½ teaspoon dry mustard
1 tablespoon molasses
2 tablespoons brown sugar
¼ teaspoon paprika
¼ teaspoon salt
⅛ teaspoon pepper
Dash Tabasco sauce
2 teaspoons Worcestershire sauce
2 tablespoons lemon juice or vinegar

Place onion and garlic in a 4-cup glass measure. Cover with plastic wrap. Microwave on HIGH (100% power) for 3 minutes. Stir in all remaining ingredients and microwave, uncovered, on HIGH for 5 minutes, stirring twice.

For immediate use: Ladle into desired jar or container. Seal or cover, and refrigerate up to 3 to 4 weeks.

For longer storage: Pack in freezer containers, leaving a 1-inch headspace; freeze.

To can: Pack in hot, sterile jars while sauce is hot. Process sealed jars conventionally in a boiling-water bath for 15 minutes.

Tomato Butter

A wonderful family heirloom recipe from our food-wise friend, Heather Kibbey. We've updated the recipe for microwave cooking. Do try this superb condiment with meat or use as you would catsup or chili sauce. Makes 4 pints.

5 pounds ripe tomatoes, peeled and sliced
2 cups cider vinegar
1½ teaspoons salt
¼ cup plus 1 tablespoon pickling spices
2¾ cups packed light brown sugar
3 tablespoons cornstarch
3 tablespoons water

In a 4-quart or larger microwave-safe mixing bowl place peeled, sliced tomatoes and vinegar; stir and cover. Let stand overnight.

Process tomato mixture in a blender or food processor to a puree. (You may need to do this in small batches.) Return pureed mixture to mixing bowl and add salt, stirring well. Microwave on HIGH (100% power) for 40 minutes, stirring every 10 minutes.

Place pickling spices in a muslin bag. Add brown sugar to pureed mixture, stirring well. Add spice bag to mixture. Microwave on HIGH for 40 minutes, stirring every 5 to 10 minutes.

Remove and discard spice bag. Combine cornstarch and water in a measuring cup, stirring until smooth. Add a small amount of the hot tomato mixture, one spoonful at a time, to the cornstarch mixture, stirring well. Add cornstarch mixture to larger hot tomato mixture, stirring well. Microwave on HIGH for 5 minutes; stir well. Ladle into sterile, hot containers, leaving a ½-inch headspace; seal.

For immediate use: Let cool and refrigerate. Keeps a month or more.

Classic Mango Chutney

This classically flavored chutney will remind you of the noted Major Grey's variety. Makes about 2 half-pints.

1 large ripe mango, peeled and sliced into 2-inch-long strips
⅓ cup coarsely chopped onion
2 tablespoons raisins
2 tablespoons golden raisins
¼ cup coarsely chopped red bell pepper
¼ cup light corn syrup
½ cup granulated sugar
1 tablespoon white-wine vinegar
1 tablespoon lime juice
3 cardamom pods, crushed, with hulls discarded *or*
   ½ teaspoon ground cardamom
1½ teaspoons ground ginger
½ teaspoon ground cumin
½ teaspoon salt

Place all ingredients in a 2-quart microwave-safe bowl, stirring gently to combine. Microwave on HIGH (100% power) for 3 minutes. Stir; microwave 7 minutes more, stirring every 2 to 3 minutes. Ladle into hot, sterile jars; seal.

For immediate use: Let cool and refrigerate up to 3 to 4 weeks.

For longer storage: Process half-pint jars conventionally in a boiling-water bath for 10 minutes.

Variation

Papaya, Peach, or Nectarine Chutney. Substitute 1 papaya or 2 peaches or 2 nectarines for mango. Proceed as directed.

Cranberry Chutney

Marsha Peters Johnson, the author of Gourmet Vinegars: How to Make and Cook with Them, *shared this exquisite recipe, which we adapted for microwave convenience. This beautiful, spicy, garnet-colored chutney is perfect with roasted meats or poultry, or with cream cheese and crackers. It's quickly prepared and makes a lovely gift. Makes 5 to 6 half-pints.*

2 cups whole cranberries
1 cup white, apple cider, white-wine, or cranberry vinegar
2 cups granulated sugar
2 teaspoons ground ginger
1 teaspoon ground cloves
¼ teaspoon chili powder
5 to 6 drops hot-pepper sauce
1 teaspoon salt
2 cloves garlic, minced
3 to 4 medium tart apples, peeled, cored, and diced
    (about 4 to 5 cups)
1 cup chopped nuts (almonds, pecans, or walnuts)

Finely chop cranberries in blender or food processor, adding ¼ cup of the vinegar. Combine all ingredients except apples and nuts (but including remaining ¾ cup vinegar) in a 2-quart glass batter bowl or deep 3-quart bowl. Microwave on HIGH (100% power) for 3 minutes. Stir; continue to microwave on HIGH until mixture comes to a boil (about 4 to 6 minutes). Stir in diced apples. Microwave on MEDIUM-HIGH (70% power) for 13 minutes, stirring twice to cook fruit evenly. Check consistency; mixture should be thick and evenly cooked. Add nuts; stir to mix well. Ladle into sterile containers.

For immediate use: Refrigerate up to 4 weeks.

For longer storage: Freeze, leaving 1-inch headspace. Keeps up to 6 months.

To can: Pack in hot, sterile jars, leaving a ½-inch headspace. Process jars conventionally, in a boiling-water bath, for 10 minutes.

Pineapple Chutney

This chutney is very good fresh but, like all chutneys, improves with a few weeks' aging in the refrigerator. Makes about 2 half-pints.

1 cup fresh or canned crushed pineapple, drained
1 cup coarsely chopped onion
1/4 cup raisins
1/4 cup golden raisins
3/4 cup brown sugar, packed
1/2 cup white vinegar
2 tablespoons grated fresh ginger*
1 1/2 teaspoons mustard seed
1 teaspoon turmeric
1/2 teaspoon lemon zest, slivered
1/2 teaspoon orange zest, slivered
1/4 to 1/2 teaspoon salt

Combine all ingredients in a 3- to 4-quart microwave-safe bowl. Stir and cover with plastic wrap. Microwave on HIGH (100% power) for 7 minutes, or until mixture comes to a boil, stirring every 3 minutes.

Reduce power to MEDIUM-HIGH (70%) and microwave for 5 to 7 minutes, stirring halfway through. Ladle into sterile jars and refrigerate. This chutney will keep 2 weeks in the refrigerator.

Variation

Pear Chutney. Substitute 1 cup fresh pear, peeled and diced, for the pineapple. Proceed as directed.

* Freeze whole fresh ginger before peeling or grating. It will peel more easily frozen and will be less stringy when grated. Place any leftover ginger in a plastic freezer bag and freeze until needed.

Easy Salsa

This medium-hot salsa can be made at any time of the year. If you prefer it milder or hotter, just vary the amount of jalapeño accordingly. Makes about 3 pints.

1 28-ounce can whole-pack tomatoes
2 medium onions, peeled and coarsely chopped
3 tablespoons vegetable oil
1 teaspoon garlic powder
2 tablespoons white or white-wine vinegar
1 teaspoon ground cumin
Dash salt
Dash pepper
2 4-ounce cans chopped green chili peppers
1 4-ounce can chopped jalapeño peppers

Coarsely chop tomatoes. In a large mixing bowl combine onion and vegetable oil. Microwave on HIGH (100% power) for 4 minutes, stirring several times. Add all remaining ingredients to onion, stirring to combine well. Microwave on HIGH for 3 minutes, then reduce power to MEDIUM (50%) and microwave for 20 minutes, stirring occasionally.

For immediate use: Cool to room temperature and serve, or refrigerate up to 2 weeks.

For longer storage: Let cool and pack into freezer containers, leaving a ½-inch headspace; freeze up to 6 months.

Fresh Salsa Verde

Salsa verde *is Spanish for "green sauce." It is made with tomatillos, small, sweet green tomatoes with a parchment-like covering. It's wonderful on chicken or crab enchiladas and other Mexican dishes. Makes 1 pint.*

1 pound fresh tomatillos (Remove the coverings before using.)
¾ cup chopped onion
1 green bell pepper
1 or 2 fresh jalapeño peppers*
2 tablespoons fresh cilantro leaves
2 garlic cloves, peeled
½ teaspoon granulated sugar

Peel tomatillos. Place them in a 3-quart or larger microwave-safe mixing bowl and cover with warm water. Microwave on HIGH (100% power) until mixture comes to a boil. (Time will vary depending upon the starting temperature of the water.) Reduce power to MEDIUM-HIGH (70%) and microwave for 3 minutes. Drain off water.

Wash, trim, and seed peppers. Coarsely chop tomatillos, peppers, and garlic. Combine all ingredients in a food processor or blender. If mixture is too thick, add water 1 teaspoon at a time. Process to sauce consistency. Pour into covered container. Refrigerate at least 1 hour to allow flavors to blend. Refrigerate sauce. Keeps up to 1 week.

* Vary the number of jalapeño peppers depending on the degree of hotness desired: Use 1 pepper for medium, 2 for hot. If you like a very mild salsa, substitute 1 large fresh or 2 canned green chili peppers.

Eggplant Caponata

Caponata is an Italian eggplant appetizer that is also an excellent meat accompaniment. Serve chilled or at room temperature with crackers or French or Italian bread. Makes about 4 pints.

3 large onions, coarsely chopped

2 large green bell peppers, seeded and coarsely chopped

1½ cups coarsely chopped celery

½ cup olive oil

2 large eggplants, cut into ½-inch cubes

1 teaspoon salt

1 8-ounce can tomato sauce

1 6-ounce can tomato paste

4 garlic cloves, peeled and minced

½ cup pitted black olives

½ cup pitted green olives (regular or stuffed)

½ cup red-wine vinegar

3 tablespoons granulated sugar

1 3-ounce jar capers

1½ teaspoons dried oregano

1 teaspoon pepper

1 teaspoon dried basil

Combine onion, pepper, celery, and olive oil in a 4-quart or larger microwave-safe bowl. Cover with plastic wrap. Microwave on HIGH (100% power) for 10 minutes, stirring halfway through. Reduce power to MEDIUM (50%) and cook for 10 more minutes, stirring occasionally.

Sprinkle 1 teaspoon salt over eggplant cubes. Set aside for 10 to 15 minutes. Add eggplant to onion mixture; stir. Microwave on HIGH for 30 minutes, stirring every 10 minutes. Add tomato sauce and paste, stirring to combine well. Microwave on HIGH 10 minutes.

Stir in all remaining ingredients. Microwave on HIGH power for 5 minutes.

For immediate use: Cool to room temperature and serve, or refrigerate up to 1 week.

For longer storage: Let cool and pack in freezer containers, leaving a ½-inch headspace. Freeze up to 6 months.

Marinated Mushrooms

An extremely popular appetizer or salad accompaniment that is a weight-watchers delight! Makes 1 quart.

1 pound fresh whole small mushrooms
1 small onion, peeled and sliced
1 tablespoon olive oil

Pickling brine:

⅔ cup white-wine or white or cider vinegar
⅓ cup water
1½ teaspoons pickling salt or uniodized salt
1 teaspoon fresh *or* ½ teaspoon dried chervil or parsley
1 bay leaf
8 peppercorns

Clean mushrooms and trim stem ends. Place mushrooms and onion slices in a large microwave-safe mixing bowl. Cover with plastic wrap. Microwave on HIGH (100% power) for 2 minutes; stir and re-cover. Microwave on HIGH for 2 minutes more. Drizzle olive oil over mushrooms; stir gently to coat mushrooms. Place in a clean quart jar.

Combine all pickling-brine ingredients in a 4-cup glass measure. Microwave on HIGH for 4 minutes or until mixture comes to a boil. Pour hot mixture over mushrooms. Seal jar and let cool before refrigerating. Let marinate in refrigerator for 24 hours before serving. Serve drained, with bay leaf and peppercorns removed. Keeps 1 week in refrigerator.

Beverages
and Special
Extras

T his is perhaps our most creative and unique chapter. Here you'll find such special delights as White Chocolate–Hazelnut Heaven and Creamy Russian Tea Base. Keep these in your freezer, ready for company or special moments that are ready as fast as your microwave can heat them.

The microwave oven is a moist-cooking appliance and therefore does not dry foods well. This, of course, is an advantage in everyday cooking. There are, however, a few foods that the microwave "dries" very well, such as herbs, peels, and croutons. Enjoy making your own Bouquet Garni and Fines Herbes from microwave-dried herbs.

Cranberry Tea

This colorful, caffeine-free "tea" is a year-round favorite whether served hot and steaming in a mug or iced in a tall glass. Makes 4 to 8 servings.

1 12-ounce bag fresh or frozen cranberries*
½ fresh orange, cut into chunks (optional)
3 cinnamon sticks
8 whole cloves
3 whole allspice berries
1 6-ounce can frozen orange juice concentrate
1 6-ounce can frozen lemonade concentrate
½ cup granulated sugar

Place cranberries and orange chunks in a large microwave-safe casserole or bowl. Cover with hot tap water. Add spices and cover with lid or plastic wrap. Microwave on HIGH (100% power) for 5 minutes, or until water comes to a boil. Stir, recover, and microwave on MEDIUM-HIGH (70% power) for 10 minutes. Pour cranberry mixture through a fine strainer into a large pitcher. Discard fruit and spices.

Add juice concentrates and sugar to cranberry mixture. Stir to combine. Refrigerate for 24 hours before serving. Can be frozen for longer storage.

To serve hot: Fill cup or mug with equal parts hot water and cranberry tea concentrate.

To serve cold: Fill a tall 8- to 10-ounce glass with ice cubes. Pour chilled cranberry tea concentrate over cubes and serve. Cranberry tea concentrate may be further diluted with cold water if fewer ice cubes are preferred.

　※ Frozen cranberries will take longer to come to a boil.

Rhubarb Blush Punch

A deliciously different iced cooler or punch. Makes about 1 quart concentrate or ½ gallon punch.

4 cups sliced rhubarb
2½ cups hot tap water
1 12-ounce can frozen lemonade concentrate
1 cup sugar

Combine rhubarb and hot water in a 3- to 4-quart microwave-safe bowl. Microwave on HIGH (100% power) for 15 minutes, or until rhubarb is mushy, stirring every 5 minutes. Strain well, reserving juice only. Add lemonade concentrate and sugar; mix well.

For immediate use: Refrigerate to chill thoroughly.

For longer storage: Freeze, leaving a 1-inch headspace.

To serve individually: Fill a tall 8- to 10-ounce glass with ice cubes. Pour chilled punch concentrate over cubes and serve. May be diluted a bit with additional water, if desired.

To serve as a punch: Pour chilled concentrate into a large punch bowl and add one of the following: 1 quart ice water, 1 quart cold 7-Up, or 1 quart iced tea. Add ice cubes or a block of ice as desired.

Rhubarb-Strawberry Punch. Add 1 cup fresh or frozen strawberries during the last 5 minutes of cooking time. Proceed as directed.

Homemade Lemonade

Real old-fashioned lemonade that has a refreshing taste. Makes about 1 quart concentrate or 1 gallon lemonade.

6 lemons
2 cups granulated sugar
1 quart water
Ice water

Wash lemons and trim ends. Slice lemons thickly. Discard seeds. Place lemon slices into large mixing bowl. Set aside. Place sugar, and 1 quart water in a 2-quart microwave-safe bowl; stir. Microwave on HIGH (100% power) for 8 to 10 minutes, stirring every 3 to 4 minutes, or until sugar is completely dissolved and mixture just barely begins to bubble around the edges of the bowl. *Do not boil.* Let cool. Pour sugar-water mixture over lemons. Let stand 10 to 15 minutes.

Press lemon slices with the back of a wooden spoon to extract all of the juice. Check for seeds; discard any found. Remove mixture and strain through a colander set over a large bowl or container. Cover and chill.

Chilled concentrate may be placed in freezer containers, sealed, and frozen if desired, or used immediately. When ready to serve, add ice water to concentrate to make 1 gallon of lemonade. Thinly slice 1 small lemon and add to diluted lemonade when serving or add 1 lemon slice per glass.

Creamy Russian Tea Base

A tangy, creamy, and not-so-sweet variation on the classic Russian Tea. Keep this recipe in your freezer. Makes 12 to 14 servings.

1 pint (2 cups) vanilla ice cream or ice milk
1 6-ounce can frozen orange juice concentrate
½ cup instant tea
½ cup granulated sugar
1 teaspoon ground cinnamon
½ teaspoon ground cloves

Soften ice cream in paper carton or large bowl on WARM (10% power) for 2 to 2½ minutes. In a large mixing bowl place orange juice concentrate, tea, sugar, and spices. Beat with electric mixer until well combined. Quickly beat softened ice cream into orange juice mixture until well blended. Spoon into freezer container, seal tightly, date, and label. Hold in freezer until needed.
To serve: Spoon ¼ cup tea mix into a 6- to 8-ounce mug or cup. Fill with boiling water. Stir and serve.

Sweetened Condensed Milk

Make your own for a fraction of the cost! Makes 1¾ cups.

1½ cups granulated sugar
½ cup water
½ cup (1 stick) butter or margarine
¼ teaspoon vanilla extract
2 cups instant dry milk

In a 1-quart glass measure or bowl, combine sugar, water, and butter. Microwave on HIGH (100% power) for 3½ to 4 minutes, or until mixture comes to a boil, stirring every minute. Blend in vanilla and dry milk. Beat until smooth in a blender or food processor or with an electric mixer. Let cool. Store, covered, in refrigerator up to a week.

Hot Buttered Rum Base

A classic hot drink with a creamy twist. Makes about 20 to 25 servings.

1 pint (2 cups) vanilla ice cream or ice milk
1 cup (2 sticks) butter or margarine
1 cup brown sugar
2 teaspoons ground cinnamon
½ teaspoon ground nutmeg
2 to 3 tablespoons rum or ¼ teaspoon rum extract (optional)

Soften ice cream in paper carton or large bowl on WARM (10% power) for 2 to 2½ minutes. Set aside.

In large microwave-safe mixing bowl soften butter on WARM for 3 to 4 minutes. Add brown sugar, cinnamon, and nutmeg to softened butter. Beat mixture with electric mixer until well combined and fluffy. Quickly add softened ice cream and continue to beat until well mixed. Spoon into freezer container, seal tightly, date, and label. Hold in freezer until needed. This mixture will not freeze solid.

To serve: Place 2 to 3 rounded tablespoons of Hot Buttered Rum Base in a cup or mug. Add rum or rum extract, if desired. Pour boiling water over all, stirring well to combine. Serve immediately.

Rich Hot Chocolate Base

This quick and easy basic hot chocolate recipe is a versatile performer. From your freezer base it can be transformed into five different and delicious hot beverages. Makes about 18 servings.

1 pint (2 cups) vanilla ice cream or ice milk
½ cup unsweetened cocoa powder
2½ cups confectioners' sugar
½ cup powdered nondairy creamer

Soften ice cream in paper carton or large bowl on WARM (10% power) for 2 to 2½ minutes. Add remaining ingredients to softened ice cream and beat well with electric mixer. Transfer to freezer container. Freeze until ready to serve.

To serve: Place 2 to 3 tablespoons Rich Hot Chocolate Base in a 6- to 8-ounce cup or mug. Fill with boiling water and stir. Top with marshmallow or whipped cream if desired.

Base Variations:

Cinnamon Hot Chocolate. Add 2 teaspoons ground cinnamon to ingredients' list and proceed as directed.

Mint Hot Chocolate. Add 2 teaspoons mint extract to ingredients' list and proceed as directed.

Serving Variations:

Chocolate-Mint Dessert Coffee. Use Mint Hot Chocolate Base recipe, substituting hot coffee for boiling water when preparing individual servings. Elegant when topped with sweetened whipped cream.

Mocha Dessert Coffee. Use Cinnamon Hot Chocolate Base recipe, substituting hot coffee for boiling water when preparing individual servings. Garnish with sweetened whipped cream and dust lightly with ground cinnamon.

Dried Herbs

A number of herbs, such as basil, celery leaves, chervil, chives, dill, mint, oregano, parsley, sage, tarragon, and thyme, may be quickly dried in your microwave oven.

1 small bunch fresh herbs (about 4 to 5 stalks)

Discard any discolored or decayed leaves. Rinse herbs in cold water; shake off excess. Pat completely dry.

Place a double layer of paper towels* in microwave oven. Spread herbs on paper towels. Place another paper towel over herbs. Microwave on HIGH (100% power) for 2 to 3 minutes. Check leaves for dryness by rubbing between paper towels to crumble. If leaves are not dry, microwave an additional 30 seconds at a time until dry. Remove from microwave oven and allow to cool. Crumble herbs, discard any tough stems, and store in an air-tight container.

* Do not use recycled paper towels; they may contain impurities such as metal particles, which could ignite the paper.

Fines Herbes

A delicate blend of herbs suitable for sauces, cream soups, stocks, fish chowders, chicken, and cheese and egg dishes. Makes a gourmet gift!

Blend equal amounts of dried chervil, chives, parsley, and tarragon. Place 1 or 2 teaspoons of mixture in a small muslin bag or a square of cheesecloth tied with kitchen string. Loop string for easy removal after cooking. Place bags in a dry airtight jar and store until needed.

Bouquet Garni

These flavorful herb packets are treasures in your soups or stews and make lovely gifts. Makes 4 bags.

2 tablespoons each dried basil, marjoram, parsley, thyme
1 tablespoon coarsely crushed bay leaves
8 cracked black peppercorns

Place about 2 teaspoons of mixture in a small muslin bag or a square of cheesecloth tied with kitchen string. Loop string for easy removal after cooking. Place bags in a dry airtight jar and store until needed.

Herb or Garlic Butter

A great make-ahead sauce for hot vegetables; or try spreading it on bread before broiling. Suggested herbs are chives, Italian parsley, rosemary, and thyme — or try one of your favorites. Mild elephant garlic or fresh shallots are also delicious. Makes ¼ cup.

¼ cup (½ stick) butter or margarine
1 teaspoon finely minced fresh herbs or garlic
1 teaspoon lemon juice

Place all ingredients in a 1-cup glass measure. Microwave on MEDIUM-HIGH (70% power) for 1 minute. Stir. Use immediately or cover and refrigerate for later use.

Basic Croutons

Vary the taste of your croutons by using different types of bread, such as French, sourdough, whole-wheat, and rye. Makes 3 cups.

3 cups fresh ½-inch bread cubes, trimmed
2 to 3 tablespoons oil or melted butter or margarine

Line a 2- to 3-quart glass baking dish with paper towels.* Spread bread cubes over paper towels evenly in a single layer. Microwave on HIGH (100% power) for 2 minutes. Stir to rearrange bread cubes and continue to cook for 1 to 2 minutes more, stirring every 30 seconds. Remove from microwave oven and let stand, uncovered, until cool. Check croutons for crispness. If necessary, cook in additional 30-second increments until crisp.

Remove paper towels and drizzle oil or melted butter over croutons. Stir to coat evenly. Serve or store in an airtight container.

Variations

Low-Sodium, Low-Fat Croutons. Substitute low-sodium bread and omit oil, butter, or margarine. Follow Basic Crouton directions.

Cheese-Garlic Croutons: Combine 3 tablespoons Parmesan cheese with ¼ to ½ teaspoon garlic powder; set aside. Follow Basic Crouton directions. Sprinkle cheese-garlic mixture over croutons after the oil or melted butter has been added and while croutons are still warm. Stir well to coat evenly.

Herbed Croutons. Use 1 teaspoon herbs per cup of bread cubes. Follow Basic Crouton directions. Add oil as directed, then immediately add 1 teaspoon herbs (try basil, chervil, chives, marjoram, oregano, parsley, tarragon, or thyme) and stir to coat evenly. You may wish to add garlic or onion powder to your herb mixture.

* Do not use recycled paper towels; they may contain impurities such as metal particles, which could heat and ignite the paper.

Festive Cheese Crock

An easy make-ahead appetizer for entertaining. Use fresh or microwave-dried herbs in the herb variation. The flavor improves with aging, but it may be used immediately. Serve with fresh round vegetable slices or crackers. Makes about 1 pint.

4 cups (1 pound) grated medium or sharp cheese
6 ounces cream cheese
2 tablespoons brandy or port
2 tablespoons plus ½ to 1 teaspoon olive oil
½ teaspoon garlic powder
1 teaspoon dry mustard

Place cheese in a large glass bowl. Microwave for 4 to 6 minutes on MEDIUM (50% power) or until soft, stirring after 2 minutes. Stir in the remaining ingredients, except the ½ to 1 teaspoon olive oil. Beat with a mixer until thoroughly blended. Pour reserved olive oil in crock. Spread evenly over crock interior. Pack cheese mixture in crock and cover with a tight-fitting lid. Refrigerate 1 week to age before serving. Serve at room temperature. Store 3 to 4 weeks in refrigerator.

Variation

Herbed Festive Cheese Crock. Layer fresh or dried herbs (basil, chervil, chives, cilantro, fines herbes, or parsley) onto cheese mixture when packing into crock: Divide cheese mixture into three equal amounts. Place first layer into crock; pat down evenly. Place 1 teaspoon dried herbs or about that amount of fresh herbs, leaves, or sprigs over top of cheese. Repeat, ending with herbs on top. Place ½ teaspoon olive oil over top of herbs. Cover and refrigerate as directed.

Roasted Pumpkin Seeds

Here's a lively condiment for salads, vegetables, and casseroles. Try this recipe with Danish or butternut squash seeds as well—crunchy and delicious! Makes about 1 cup.

1 cup pumpkin seeds
Salt
½ teaspoon oil (optional)

Rinse fibers from pumpkin seeds; drain. Sprinkle a light coating of salt on a microwave baking tray or shallow dish. Place damp seeds in a single layer on the salt. Drizzle ½ teaspoon oil over seeds, if desired. Microwave, uncovered, on HIGH (100% power) for 6 to 7 minutes, stirring once halfway through cooking time. Taste-test seeds for crispness. Microwave 1 to 2 minutes more if needed. Store in a sealed container.

White Chocolate–Hazelnut Heaven

A stunning and versatile preparation that can be used as a fondue, a drizzle topping, a pâté, or, if allowed to harden, a confection.

For a heavenly fondue, dip fresh fruits in the mixture while still liquid (especially good with fresh berries). Or simply drizzle the mixture over a fruit plate. To serve as a pâté, let cool to firm and spread on firm fruits, fruit slices, or specialty breads. To make elegant confections, dip whole small fruits, such as strawberries or cherries with stems attached, into hot fondue. Place on plate and chill until firm. Serve chilled. Easy to make and ready at a moment's notice from your freezer. Makes about 4 cups.

3 cups (14-ounces) white chocolate chips or
  finely chopped white chocolate
¾ cup whipping cream or half-and-half
½ cup finely chopped toasted hazelnuts*
1 tablespoon hazelnut liqueur *or* 1½ teaspoons almond
  or black walnut extract
½ teaspoon vanilla extract

Place white chocolate in a 2-quart glass batter or mixing bowl and microwave for 1 minute on HIGH (100% power). Set aside.

Place cream in a 1-cup glass measure and microwave on HIGH for 1 to 1½ minutes, or just until cream reaches a boil. While cream is being microwaved, stir white chocolate to blend. Pour hot cream over melted chocolate. Add hazelnuts, liqueur, and vanilla extract. Stir to mix well.

For immediate use: Pour into container(s) and refrigerate up to 4 weeks.

For longer storage: Freeze, leaving a ½-inch headspace.

* Hazelnuts are also known as filberts.

Glossary of Preserving Terms

Ascorbic Acid: the chemical name for vitamin C. Lemon and pineapple juice contain large quantities of ascorbic acid and are commonly used to prevent browning of peeled, light-colored fruits and vegetables.

Conserve: a mixture of several fruits, cooked to a jamlike consistency with sugar, and often with nuts and raisins.

Cooking down (also known as jamming): a technique that uses no thickener—such as pectin—but thickens naturally by slowly cooking for a longer period of time until desired consistency is reached.

Dry pack: a technique that does not require any added liquids or sugar when preparing fruits—such as blueberries—for freezing.

Fruit Butter: a thick, smooth spread made by cooking pureed fruit pulp with sugar and spices.

Headspace: the unfilled space above food or liquid in jars or freezing containers. Allows for food expansion as jars are heated or containers are frozen, and for forming vacuums as jars cool.

Herb or Spice bag: a closeable fabric, usually made of unbleached muslin, that is used to extract herb and spice flavors in a pickling solution or in cooking.

Jam: a preserve of whole fruit, slightly crushed, cooked with sugar until thick.

Jelly: a clear, transparent preserve that retains its shape when unmolded. Made by cooking a clear liquid (usually fruit juice) with sugar.

Jelly bag: usually made of unbleached muslin. They may be purchased where canning supplies are sold. It is used in the final straining of fruit juices for maximum clarity of the jelly. Squeezing the bag can cause cloudy jelly.

Marmalade: a clear, jellylike preserve with fruit (usually citrus) suspended in small pieces or thin slices.

Peel: the entire rind, skin, or covering of a fruit.

Pickling: a method of adding enough vinegar or lemon juice to low-acid foods to lower the pH to 4.6 or lower. Properly pickled foods may be safely heat-processed in a boiling-water bath.

Pickling Salt: also called canning salt. This is regular table salt without the anti-caking or iodine additives.

Preserves: fruit or pieces of fruit, cooked with sugar until tender and plump. The fruit remains whole and the syrup becomes transparent and very thick.

Wet pack: a general term that includes both hot and cold pack methods when a liquid is added to the fruit or vegetable before preserving by either freezing or canning.

Zest: the thin and delicate outside layer of the rind or skin of a fruit.

Index